Don't Be Invisible Be Fabulous
Volume 8

Worthy For More

Compiled by

Dorris Burch

Don't Be Invisible Be Fabulous, Volume 8:
Worthy For More

Copyright © 2022 Dorris Burch

Published by Fab Factor Publishing
Tinley Park, IL
www.thefabfactor.com

ISBN: 978-0-578-39101-4

Cover design, layout, and typesetting:
Fab Factor Publishing

Cover photo: Orlett W Photography

This book is for every woman to remember…

Don't Be Invisible. Be Fabulous!

CONTENTS

The Fabulous
Dorris Burch

INTRODUCTION

Can I get real with you for a moment? (Oh who am I kidding—you know I get down and dirty with the truth without permission, right? That's just my style.)

I know sometimes we women just share the FAB stuff, but I want to share my story of the not-so-fab, not-so-cool stuff. Personally, I think we need to share more of these truths so that we can heal from those un-truths that whisper things like "You're not as good as her" "Look at how amazing she's doing compared to you" "She's lucky and I'm not"

Ever felt those whispers?

I sure have. But the truth is, we ALL have gone through our battles, and I for sure, had a lot to heal before I stepped more fully into my FAB shoes being me.

Ok, so here it goes… truth-telling time…

Just a couple years ago, I was stuck. I felt trapped in my prison of doubt and fear. And the thing that caused me tons of emotional pain was feeling like I had all these gifts and dreams, but not feeling sure if I could (or would) ever create them.

I was scared that I would never truly live up to my full potential.

I had these two opposing forces fighting with each other in my body. Once force said, "Yes! I'm a Light. There's a rockstar within me! I am meant to shine and lead and create my desires AND get paid well" And then at the same time, this other force kicked in and told me to just stay hidden. Most of the time, when it came to following through on my desires of being a leader, I had a fear of really being seen and heard as my true self. I couldn't (wouldn't) speak on the things I wanted to talk about in public.

When I spoke about what I love and lights me up, I felt like my heart would leap out of my chest... I had dreams of leading workshops, of stepping on stages, of creating a movement... but how could I do those things????

The fabulous news is that today I'm doing just that. And I love it!

I share this with you because I've noticed quite a lot these past few years and I see all of you AMAZING leaders. And yet, so many women share with me that they do not fully own their power, they're not really leading in the way they want, or being seen in the spotlight the way they want, or creating the money they want.

In short, they're not claiming the badass visionary fabulous woman within. If this is you, I get it. As I said, I've sooooooooo been there. And take it from a once shy girl, trapped in a box... you can totally step into the powerful leader within to be seen and heard in your biz and personal life (and make money from your movement/message/leader-self if that's what you want!)

I know you can have that. If you're part of my tribe and community it's because you _are_ a badass leader! And I want to support you as fully as I can, so you can totally own the rock star within and live like the BVFW that you are.

See if this definition of a BVFW (Badass Visionary Fabulous Woman) resonates with you...

1. A woman that owns her worth and receives abundantly for her fabulousness
2. A woman that is clear on her vision and creates from her desires
3. A woman that stands in her truth and is able to speak it

What do you think? Do you resonate with that definition? If you DO resonate and at the same time feel a little shaky in one of those three areas (or in all 3 areas like I once did!) you do NOT want to confine yourself. We use constraints in our own lives. We jail our spirit by allowing these 2 things to get in our own way...

Doubt and fear.

We're struck with brilliance—literally--the seed of inspiration hits us, inspiration talks to us, and BAM we get a super-uber-cool idea. We're inspired, we're enthralled, we're entranced, we see the Light... and what do we do? A lot of times we stop-- before we've even gotten started. Doubt and fear appear... and power disappears. The very power we feel when there is an absence of constraint in choice... is gone. Ladies, when will we stop jailing ourselves? When will the second guessing stop?

You are in your most powerful place when you follow through on inspiration despite any doubt or fear.

See, if you don't act on YOUR inspired ideas, sooner or later that jolt of inspiration will knock less and less. And then you'll miss out on that yummy feeling of reveling in your freedom, of living without constraint.

But here's the good news, no matter where you're at in your fierce freedom factor, you can always bring it back.

Here's 4 easy steps to claiming a high score on your owning and living in your power:

1. Stop and notice when you get even a tiny twinge of inspiration.

2. Instead of passing that feeling up and saying "I'm too busy" or "That's too crazy" or "What will other people think?" try asking yourself this… Is this a fun, exciting, make-my heart flutter, joyful idea? If it is, move on to the next step…

3. Imagine how stepping into this idea will help you grow as a person and claim your fabulousness as a woman (cuz you're allowed to be powerful, in fact I say it's your Goddess Given Birthright)

4. Take action on your inspired idea. Go for it, my sister. Run. Dance. Fly. And watch as you become a POWERFUL woman.

Today I give you permission to own your power by taking action on your inspired wild ideas!

I know that it is time for women like you to go bold, big, and badass. We see too many amazing leaders still playing small-- in the money area, in the "taking a stand for your truth" area, and in the area of truly being seen and voicing your beautiful truth.

So if you're ready to create a movement in the world, make the money you want, or simply become the leader of your own life… join us!

Remember –

Don't Be Invisible. Be Fabulous!

The Fabulous Dorris Burch

Janyne
Szklaruk

BELIEVE YOU DESERVE IT AND THE UNIVERSE WILL SERVE IT

Where does one begin to tell their story? What part of it is meant to be shared? What part will others resonate with? Because now, at 45 years old, I know that no one gets this far without being hurt, traumatized, scarred. It's life, beautiful and tragic.

What makes my story special? In truth, nothing. Nothing makes my story more special or more important than your story. I am writing this because I know that I must share it, not because it's important, but because maybe it can give someone the belief that they, too, can design their life to be more! More of whatever it is they desire.

Beginnings are a strange thing, aren't they? Some feel momentous right from the get-go, yet others feel necessary. Either way, I realize now, more than ever, that life is filled with new beginnings. It is my intention that by sharing my story, my journey, others can find the hope and deep belief that they, too, can get through the challenges, tragedies, and heartaches of life and still be grateful, abundant, and joyous.

The way I see it, we can all use a reminder that it all comes down to a series of beginnings and endings, one after the other. And, at least for me, without fail, the moment I feel like I've gotten to a point where I can hit cruise control, take my foot off the gas or take a break for even a split second, the tide turns, and we're right back to another new beginning, sometimes grand, sometimes insignificant.

Not so long ago, I would have written a different story. I would have shared with you how I was raised, how my beliefs were shaped, and how the expectations placed on me created my life. Now, I get to share with you that *because* of those things, it shaped my life. So, let me go back to those things that I was forever holding on to as an excuse.

I am proud of my upbringing. Born and raised on a farm and ranch in rural Alberta, Canada, I had a very cool childhood. We worked hard, but played hard too. I am the middle of five kids whose ages were all incredibly close (six and a half years from oldest to youngest). Our family life was hectic and chaotic, but it didn't feel like it at the time. I loved that my only-child best friend gravitated towards our craziness, and I loved going to her calm and quiet household. I had everything I wanted and more. Growing up in the middle of nowhere, surrounded by wide open prairies in every direction, I somehow still always felt like I was somewhat closed in. While I loved my childhood, the older I got, the more I dreamed of a life bigger than anything I knew around me.

After I graduated high school at 18, I packed up and moved away to college, with big dreams just waiting to burst out. But what happened was that by 20, feeling enormous family and societal expectations, I ended up married. With a husband and two beautiful kids by the time I was 25, we had a really nice life, but I always knew something was missing in my soul.

By deciding to marry at 20 years old, I believed I could *will* myself to be happy. I married under pressure of "not living in sin," but deep down, I knew it was not what I wanted. I decided I had no choice but to "do the right thing" and, by doing so, was righteous and good. I didn't even allow myself to look at what else could be possible. Gosh, that 20-year-old me had believed the thinking in my head that this would be good enough!

I am grateful to this day that I married a good guy. He was a good husband, and a good dad. He loved me, and I loved him, but I wasn't *in* love with him, and I wasn't in love with the life we were living. I had been living with the perpetual turmoil of trying to make myself happy with the life I was living but constantly having a pull towards a truly epic, fulfilling life. But I didn't know how to change my situation, so I tolerated my life as it was and clung to hope that things would be different one day. I'd either learn to accept it, or somehow, my life would magically fill all of my desires.

Fast forward to about age 30, and I felt disempowered and underwhelmed with my predictable life, and my soul ached for more. I had followed all the rules; I did everything right. I was willing to work hard, pay bills, and be good to others. I went to church. I put my family first, all the things we are conditioned to do. My "epic" life was feeling stuck, trapped. I was sad because nothing ever really changed. I saw no way out, and I believed that I was stuck with the decision I had made at 20 years old. I wondered if my life was meant to be this heavy. I was not thriving, and life felt disenchanted. I was a "good wife," a "good mom," a "good woman." I was all I had been programmed to be. Yet, even as my soul grew heavier, I never completely gave up on my dream and desire for an epic life.

I WAS MODELING A LIFE OF ACCEPTANCE

But here is where the true catalyst for change was: I was sitting in the hot tub one evening when my 10-year-old son said to me, "Mom, how come when Dad kisses you, you never kiss him back?" Wow! At that moment, I knew I owed more to my kids, and my husband deserved better.

It became clear to me that I was modeling a life of acceptance, and status quo, mediocrity, and settling for sensible. I knew that I had to do something different in my soul at that moment. I had never actually considered that leaving the marriage might actually be better, that I might *be* better, and that I had an opportunity to show my kids that they did not have to settle for ordinary. Instead, I could show them that it is their responsibility to themselves to trust their own desires and live a fulfilling life of their own choosing. I had the opportunity to model compassionate change and give them permission to live a fulfilled life in a healthy relationship.

At some point, I decided I needed to stop giving

power to other people's expectations. I needed to decide what I wanted, and this was just the beginning of the end. I wish I could say that the next part was easy, painless, and quick, but it was a process. I had decided I would be leaving that marriage, but I hadn't yet figured out the details of when or how. I felt like I needed to find the best way to leave as gracefully as possible, given the devastation that would be left behind. In the meantime, I also decided to do my best to maintain my false happiness and carry on until I could figure it all out.

You could say I was procrastinating, but I was planning. And so many times, my thoughts tried to convince me that I was better off just staying, that everyone would be better off if I just stayed and made it work, that I should sacrifice my dreams and desires not to disrupt the happiness of those around me. I had so much to work through in my brain, and the push/pull was relentless. But as days turned into months and months into years, I finally reached my crossroads. I actually picked a leave date and went to work behind the scenes, getting our life in order. We had a farm and a business and debt. I wanted to be sure that I could support myself when I left, and my husband would financially survive, too. I didn't want half of everything; I wanted to leave peacefully and with as little trauma as possible. I wanted him to keep our home so our kids would have that. So we sold our land but kept the house and 5 acres around it, sold the business and paid off nearly all of our debt. At this point, I had confided in my husband what I was planning. He was devastated and truly believed we could fix our marriage. Not that we actually had anything "wrong" with it, specifically, but I don't think he could really see what was going on deep below the surface. It wasn't him as ironic as it sounds; it really *was* me.

As the date I picked got closer, I had secured a small rental home in town where I would move. Our marriage counselor was helping us through mediation and child arrangements, and we agreed upon shared custody, alternating weeks. This process was so very difficult, and I wish I could say that we navigated it with grace and respect, but we definitely had moments of anger, hurt, heartache, and, dare I say, even hate. It was so very hard. Yet, not a day went by that I didn't have thoughts just to concede and go back to what would be the easy road and stay.

After 14 years of marriage, it was over, and the day we told the kids I was leaving would forever be one of the hardest days of my life. As I write this, all the emotions and heartache that I experience are rushing back as sharp as they were then… There were devastated, innocent little faces, and tears, not to mention the heartache I was causing, brought me to my knees; I almost couldn't bear it. I prayed so hard that I would forgive myself one day for wanting more and that those impacted would forgive me one day, too.

This decision affected so many more than just our immediate household. Our families were devastated. Our friends were devastated. It came as a huge surprise to most. We hadn't confided in many, and those who I had, I think, assumed that there was no way I'd leave what was a good and comfortable life. Something I did not expect was that I would be shunned, shamed, and hurt by those closest to me. I realize now it was a reflection of them and how they were processing it all and their own limiting beliefs. But it hurt me deeply. My mom did not support my decision, and she didn't accept it for quite some time. Because she is a devout Catholic, divorce wasn't an option in her opinion, and I had to respect that she didn't accept my decision. I have friends who have barely spoken to me since. But, again, I realize now it wasn't about me, except that my decision likely made them look inside themselves and perhaps didn't like what they saw.

I left that marriage because I knew there was more for me beyond that comfortable life in my heart. I had settled. Settled for not thinking for myself, settled for living by the rules that others imposed upon me, and failing to be true to what was possible for me.

I FEEL EMPOWERED AND BRAVE

It is hard to look back at that period without angst and regret at all the hurt and heartache I caused. But when I retell it, I feel empowered and brave. It feels courageous when I realize that I didn't just continue to settle for the mediocre life that I had once chosen. It feels powerful that I did something so hard, on my own, that not one person in my life understood, and I rose up on the other side of it all.

There was a point in that transitional time when I knew I owed it to myself. But equally important to me was that I owed it to my little humans to show them that they did not have to settle for a life of circumstance or mediocrity, but they could design a life they desired. Through this whole process, I kept going back to the belief that things always have a way of working out, even when we don't yet see it. And at the end of that chapter of my life was the start of so many new beginnings. Big and small.

Only a few months after I had left my then-husband, I started seeing someone I had met several months earlier through mutual friends. Yes, I get that the timing was not ideal, especially in the minds of others. But, again, those around me were casting judgment around their beliefs that I had moved on too soon, that I wasn't even trying to save my marriage. Little did they know that my decision to leave my marriage happened long before I physically left. I had emotionally moved on long before I moved out. In the process of leaving my marriage, one thing I had done was think a lot about my future and what I actually wanted and desired. I was prepared to be alone and knew I was capable and strong enough to be alone too. I had read the book The Secret not long before I had left my marriage, which changed how I looked at life. I would no longer allow life to happen to me, but I would take charge and start creating the life I desired. And so, I had also made a list of all the things I desired in a true partner in the future.

You know how it goes; we don't get to decide the timing of the universe, but what did happen was that I manifested my perfect partner to show up a lot sooner than I had expected! He showed up and was exactly what I manifested. I once again had to fight with the martyr in me, saying, "you can't be in a new relationship yet, especially a serious one." I had to trust that the timing was divine, regardless of others' thoughts. This new relationship was exactly as it was meant to be, and it wasn't long before I knew this was the relationship that I had always dreamed and desired.

With this new relationship came all kinds of new obstacles and challenges. First, of course, I had two small humans who needed to be considered. And then there was all the resistance around us, but I will forever be grateful that he fought for us. He embraced my kids as a part of me, and instead of choosing an easier relationship without the baggage, he chose us, and he still does today.

This new relationship brought so much belief back to my life that all of the hurt and heartache were just part of the process to get to my epic life. At this point, I am 36 years old, and we decided that we would like to have some children together. This was a tough decision for me because my older kiddos were now 10 and 12, and the thought of starting over seemed overwhelming. But I also knew that there were no rules and that I needed to follow my desire, and so we chose to have a baby out of wedlock! Again, against so many people in our lives and their beliefs, we didn't want to wait, just to make sure we were doing things in the "right order" and married before having a child. This was a conscious choice, and ironically, announcing that we were pregnant and having a baby is actually what repaired the relationship with my mom, who wanted to have a relationship with this new grandbaby.

We did not see it coming that our daughter would be

born with some significant health challenges that challenged us in so many ways. We had no warning or awareness that anything was wrong until hours after her birth, when they discovered that she could not swallow. We spent the following days and months in the NICU with her while the doctors searched for answers everywhere, never finding the cause of her dysphagia (the inability to swallow).

We brought her home from the hospital with a feeding tube and a short training for us to learn how to change it, put it back in, and care for her on our own. We had no real answers, only told that she would have her feeding tube until she was a young adult. I have to admit that this was such a trying time for me, and it was hard to accept that this was going to be not only her fate but ours as well. Thankfully, I had some life experience as a mom at this point in my life, and I researched online until we found a clinic in Austria that specialized in weaning tube-fed babies. At 15 months old, we launched into the program via the internet, and eight days later, she was 100% weaned off her feeding tube. Now at nine years old, she is happy and healthy. Meanwhile, I felt as though I had abandoned all of my epic dreams to become her primary caregiver. While I loved being at home and available to my family, I felt like I had lost my purpose and the desire for more, and I struggled to embrace this new role.

Shortly after overcoming all of that, we learned we were expecting another child. When we had our daughter, I had known that we should have at least one more sibling close in age since there was such an age gap between her and my older children, and I didn't want this youngest one to be like an "Only" child. It was perfect timing, and these two babies would be exactly 21 months apart, the exact difference between my two oldest kids, and this baby was due on my new husband's 30th birthday! We were so excited to be completing our little blended family.

But, at our regular scheduled 20-week ultrasound, we received devastating news. The next few days were a blur as we went to several specialists who confirmed that the baby we were carrying had trisomy13, a terminal condition. We were counseled by many and given all of our options. And every single choice we were given was going to be tragic and heartbreaking. My brain could barely function. But, there wasn't one choice that would be easier than another. I couldn't even believe this was happening, and to this day, it still feels like the worst imaginable nightmare, only we were living it.

I had so much internal, ethical and moral turmoil that it physically made me sick for days. We had wanted this baby so badly. But to know that carrying him to term could be the worst possible suffering for him was the most painful. I never imagined that I would have to make a choice to let go of my child. First, I had to trust my faith in God, that He would accept our decision. Then, I could accept our decision.

Several days later, we got a call that there was a bed available for my induction so that we could peacefully deliver this precious baby. I have never experienced more trauma in my life, laboring to deliver a baby that would be stillborn. To be frank, it was a horrific experience that I was not prepared for in any way, shape or form. My body did not respond to induction, and it took almost two days for the delivery.

I had decided I could forgive myself for the decision we made, knowing that it was the right decision, but the moment Burke was born, I thought I was going to die with a broken heart. I immediately questioned why I hadn't just allowed nature to take its course? Why had we intervened? Why was this happening to me? Did I deserve this heartache? Why? Why? Why?

But, there was one thing that gave me relief and comfort in that moment, and that was when they passed his tiny body to me, and he had such a beautiful peace about him. He was so, so precious and perfect, and I knew that we saved him from suffering.

Throughout my life, when we've lost people closest to us, I remember my mom often said, there are worse things than death. I was raised to have a strong faith in God, and in those moments, I recall having a knowing that there are indeed worse things than death. But the reality was that we loved that baby from the moment we knew he existed, and we lost so many hopes and dreams when we lost him. And on top of it all was the pain of regret of a decision we couldn't turn back from. I know I saved him from suffering, but I didn't know then that the suffering would transfer to me. It has taken years now of my own suffering to work through this heartache and pain. So, on one hand, I know we made the right decision, but on the other hand, I will always wonder.

In hindsight, I regret not having asked for more help. We tried to navigate all this without having to bring more heartache to the people who loved us most. After all, we had each other. But the reality was that the burden was too big to carry, and it shattered me to my core. Looking back now, it was a selfish decision not to allow our loved ones in closer to help us through it all because our loss was their loss, too. Our heartache was their heartache. But I truly had no idea the impact it would have on me.

Here we are, almost eight years later, and I know that our life is as it was meant to be. We lost with Burke's death, but we also gained so much. We grew. We are living and celebrating life because we know all too well that life is fragile. I still have moments where the pain comes rushing back. I have moments where it feels so fresh, so heavy, but most days, I find a reason to smile at the memory of that little soul who came for just a short time. That little soul had the biggest impact on my heart and life, and I am grateful that his short existence made such significance every day.

I JUST DECIDED TO SAVE MYSELF

During this traumatic time, I found myself struggling with the grief that was consuming me, day in and day out. I felt myself spiraling downwards into a depression that I knew wasn't healthy, but I also had no idea how to stop it, except that I just decided to save myself one random day.

One thing I knew was that I needed a distraction from it all, and the only thing I knew that I could consume myself in was some kind of work or project or something that got me excited. So I went online and Googled "work from home." A company popped up that was launching in Canada the very next day. I took that as a sign from the universe, and I immediately said yes to it!

I had no idea about any of it. It was an entirely new industry that I knew nothing about. It really was a huge leap of faith but what I immediately found was an incredible community of others who lifted me up, supported me, and helped me through my healing process, all the while I started earning money! I felt like I had purpose again.

I thought I could make a few hundred dollars a month and feel like I was contributing again but, I learned quickly that I was dreaming much too small. I realized so much more was possible, including creating a six-figure a year income from our tiny rural town in southern Alberta. It filled every gap that I was looking for in my life and in a business and now allows the time and financial freedom that I had always imagined my traditional business would allow. Only now, I get to be fulfilled around my family, working from home, and helping others create the life they desire to. That one leap of faith created so many options and choices for our family.

I think having the experience of losing a child brought a deeper desire to stop playing small. To truly live an epic life. It was just four years ago now that we were driving home from a weekend at our lake property that I asked my husband, "if you could live anywhere, where would it be?" We started to contemplate moving to a different community once the two oldest kids were in college because we had to stay in our small town to maintain shared custody of the older kids with their dad. But because it was the community I had lived in my entire first marriage, it always felt like I became the outsider after divorcing, and Chad became a bigger outsider coming into the community. We never felt supported or accepted, and we both longed for the day when we could pack up and have a fresh start somewhere without all the judgment.

I already knew where I would go, Belize. But when he answered Belize, I knew that we had to make that happen! And so began an entirely new discovery of "why not?" We had all of the discussions around what was holding us back from doing it. It turns out nothing, except our own limiting beliefs, so we just decided we would make it happen. At the point of that decision, we had a year and a half to figure it out because we wanted to be there, settled when our youngest would be starting first grade, and the two oldest both in college. It felt like that was our window of opportunity if we were going to do something so big. So we booked a trip to the island of Ambergris Caye, where we had vacationed several times before. But this time we booked for a month so that we could experience it through the eyes of living there. While there, we would search for a home. We arrived there, got settled, and loved the idea of making our new life there. We registered our daughter in the school there, searched for a home, and acted 'as if'. The day we found the perfect property (one that was going to be a fixer-upper, just one lot back from the beach) was also the day my husband got an offer to transfer to Florida!

So here we were, at another crossroads with a huge decision to make. In the end, I realized that by putting it out to the universe that we were moving somewhere warm and tropical, the universe brought us our perfect opportunity, which would be in Florida. Six months later, we had sold our home in Canada, sold nearly everything we owned, dissolved our home construction business, and we packed up in one 20 'trailer with a minimal amount of our belongings and moved almost 4000 miles to Florida. In hindsight, this is exactly where we needed to be because, eight months after moving, COVID shut down the world, and we were separated from our families on the other side of the border. However, I cannot imagine how hard it would have been to be stuck on an island with no way out.

We have challenges with traveling freely back and forth to Canada now, but it has been possible throughout the pandemic, just not ideal. We have been in Florida now for two years. Our life here is truly the epic dream life I have always desired. I feel more empowered now to show others what is possible when we live true to our desires.

All of my new beginnings were stepping stones on the path that led me to learn, grow, and stand in my power today. I have learned to manifest and attract incredible things and people in my life, living a life that I am creating instead of living a life that I accepted.

I stopped giving power to what others deemed acceptable. If I had continued to live the life that was deemed acceptable, sensible, and responsible, my epic life would never have happened. Instead, I now wake up thrilled and excited to be living out my true desires and purpose.

You cannot fast forward through the hard stuff in

business and life. Just as change has been a constant in my story, there are seasons--good and bad--but with willingness and grit, you can do things to control how you respond and work harder than whatever is working against you! I only recently really and truly have understood that everything in my life happened FOR me, not TO me. What a deep revelation!. And why did it take me so long for this to register? I have heard this so many times, but it never sunk in and triggered anything in me for some reason. Until now.

Knowing this has helped set me free. Knowing this has allowed me to see things differently. To forgive. To stop the blame and excuses that I didn't even know I was holding on to. I suddenly get that it all happened FOR me and because I attracted it. I trust the process of life to be on my side. I realize I have the power to manifest my desires, and so do you!

Janyne
Xoxo

ACKNOWLEDGMENTS

I am deeply thankful for so much in my life. First and foremost, to my incredibly supportive husband Chad, who is everything I ever dreamed of in a partner. To my kids, Quaid, Tory and Kemery who inspire me to rise above always. To my parents, who raised me to believe that I was capable of getting through all that life could serve me. Lastly, I am filled with hope that by sharing my story, you are reminded that even if you don't fully understand, your journey is meant for you.

ABOUT AUTHOR

Janyne has been an entrepreneur her entire adult life. She is driven with a passion to show others that they, too, can design a life that rises above the mediocrity that society expects and manifest into a life they love. She has created the website, This Well-thy Life, which encompasses a life exemplified by abundance, happiness, purpose, health and joy. Janyne has also built a thriving organization and is a top earner in her network marketing company. She enjoys the industry, and is inspired by mentoring and coaching her team, watching them discover the freedom that the business allows. Born and raised in Alberta Canada, Janyne and her husband Chad, sold most everything they owned, packed up the rest and moved their family to South Florida in 2019, where they enjoy the life they once only imagined.

ABOUT MY BUSINESS

Janyne is partnered with a leading health & wellness company. She is also a mentor and coach helping those on her team achieve their dreams.

Website
www.thiswellthylife.com

Facebook Personal Page
https://www.facebook.com/janyne.szklaruk/

Instagram
https://instagram.com/janyneszklaruk/

THANK YOU!

ALLOW ME TO SHARE THE WELL-TH WITH YOU! From $10 off your first order to tips, tricks and other resources to help you discover your well-thy life! www.thiswellthylife.com

The chalkboard reads:

HONESTY
ENTREPRENEURIAL CAPITALIST
INTEGRITY

Meg
Schmitz

FROM CHRYSALIS TO BUTTERFLY: STRONG, POWERFUL WOMAN

When Dorris asked me to contribute to her latest book, I immediately said yes. Being asked to share my story is a pleasure and a cleansing experience, not a chore, although sometimes I worry that I will suffer from writer's block. What if I forget something?

How can one get writer's block when telling one's own story? Silly. But we all have doubts, don't we?

My name is Meg Schmitz, and I am a wife, mother, businesswoman, employer, board member, investor and mentor, conservationist, outdoor lover, and franchise fashionista. About 20 years ago, I can confidently report that I became, and still am, fabulous… and I earned every one of those letters. But, because of some epic failures.

It may seem that becoming a confident, fabulous woman is an entitlement for some women from the outside. She was born with it. She was born into it. She was hand-picked or given opportunities that others weren't. One thing I can tell you with certainty is that we ALL have a unique journey, and thus a story to tell. We are birthed into this world the same way, but our living conditions, parenting, and then our own choices provide the platform for our future. Success or failure, and everything in between, is a mindset and ours to choose. Life is not always fair or easy, and we need to groom and train our minds because life is a marathon to prepare for and embrace success. Even women who were handed fame and fortune have been known to blow it and lose it all. Don't make me name names.

It works to fully live life, and like a happy ending, you have to experience unhappiness and tragedy before you can arrive at that happy place. I don't know anyone who got to skip challenges and that sense of frustration, failure, or unhappiness. For me, fighting the fight is what makes success so sweet. Even when you get there, it's never over, and the game never stops. Unless you're dead. If only we could all die at the crescendo, achieving some unparalleled happiness, and then the curtain comes down. But who wants it to end? It is so seductive to get into that cadence, the rhythm of achievement and winning, that we keep playing the game, upping the ante and rolling the dice. Can we continually keep winning? That is a fabulous goal, but not my experience.

Ask a football player what it's like to play a position where they are continually knocked down and must get back up again. Repeatedly. The aches and pains are part of the job, and that's how I view life. Dedicated players commit their bodies to their craft, practicing over and over again to drive toward the goal line. They are also trained to protect themselves, aggressively pursuing the opposition, so there is an accomplishment and earning THE WIN. I have felt like that football player, running into obstacles that seemed impassable. Training the body and grooming the mind are key elements to remain optimistic and recognizing opportunity when it presents itself.

Being a confident woman is a magnificent accomplishment and well worth embracing. Exuding confidence is one thing, but being a confident woman is another. There's "fake it 'til you make it," and then there is inherent confidence that doesn't shake loose. Men, and other women, can see it ooze out in your posture, smile, engagement, attitude, and ultimately your femininity. Being is a continued state, having arrived at some point and being unwilling to leave. You belong here, being recognized, elevated, and emulated. Becoming a confident woman means breaking out of the chrysalis and fluttering those strong, resilient, yet delicate and compassionate wings. Take flight, alight, and enjoy the experience and the view.

I have the pleasure of working with more women today than ever before, and the movement is not slowing down. Do they come to me confident? No. But I did not start this way, either. I am honored to be able to contribute my story to this book because my success did not get delivered to me. I wanted to be that Warrior, to become that winner who could claim a place on the stage called Success. Becoming a confident, accomplished woman had to come from trial and error, stumbles and falls, and in a couple instances EPIC FAILURES.

I WAS IN THE SHADOWS

I became that woman I envisioned I could be, and here's my story.

When I was young, I believed I was invisible. Not really invisible, just not visible to my parents. I was in the shadows, in the shallows, crowded out by my bossy, domineering brother and my younger, more bosomy, and blonde sister. My father was a renowned surgeon until his retirement, and he hangs onto that accomplishment to this day. My mother grew up in a small town with small-minded parents, wanting to become a doctor but sent, instead, to nursing school. While my dad's career took off, my mother was pressured by social standards to give up her dreams and worked as a school nurse instead. My brother had emotional issues throughout our years growing up, and my sister was demanding. I believe my mom and I were equally invisible when the nuclear family was all together. It's hard to live in a household of narcissists and gain self-confidence.

In high school, I had one boyfriend for most of those years, and he became my rock. Howard and I were quite the pair, with opposite body types and heights, but I loved, loved, LUVED him. Being a partner to him, I was finally free to live outside of those big egos and long shadows at home. We both had jobs, he played on the varsity basketball team, and together we drove his truck with a plow during the winter. We made a lot of money by unburying neighborhood driveways after Chicago snowstorms. We had a blast, and life was grand until his dad made him break up with me the summer before college (we all experience discrimination… in this case, I was not Jewish). Howard and I had a lovely reunion a couple of years ago, and we still stay in touch. In recounting the years, we reminisced about how we both found our way out of teenage isolation and into confidence. There is nothing like love to bolster your ego and help you realize that you really are meaningful to someone else. Until his dad takes it all away….

So I'll stop there reliving the early years. As I write it, it sounds like a pretty innocuous yet entitled upbringing, all in all. My surgeon dad, mom was always around, North Shore affluence, college at Northwestern. But I had a self-esteem problem that remerged my freshman year in college, the invisibility issue, and I developed anorexia. My high-school love was gone, and attending a different university, and I was floundering to find my own way. I wasn't loved, and I didn't love myself. The family dynamics with my siblings became much more complex, and we were definitely a splintered family. Those were difficult years to live through.

Anorexia is a big deal. Along with that, in my mid-20s, I developed anxiety which caused bleeding ulcers the size of silver dollars. I was trying to disappear again since I didn't seem to be important to anyone. After graduating from Northwestern, I emerged as a top sales performer in my first two careers. But it was hard to maintain that level of perfection that comes with anorexia, and I needed therapy. Now, at nearly 60, I still have lingering effects and body image issues, but now I know that I am NOT invisible. Just enviably thin and well maintained. When Dorris first interviewed me, I connected immediately with her website design and tagline. Don't Be Invisible. Be Fabulous!

So how did I become FABULOUS? It is a process!

READY, AIM, FIRE

The area of my life that gave me the greatest confidence was in helping others to become better, achieve more, and gain happiness and satisfaction with their work. I spent many years focusing on others, which is what an anorexic thinks they do best. Deny the self by giving to others. Give completely to others while depleting the self. Somewhere around 24, I figured out that I wasn't focused on others. I was focused on disappearing and realized that starving myself didn't make me a better giver or more esteemed. I was at cross purposes with myself (I didn't learn it on my own... thank years of counseling for that!). It was a process, but when I learned to nurture myself, my body and my mind were able to do more good. Abundance begets abundance.

About that same time, more or less age 24, I met my first husband through the Windy City BMW Club. The club hosts high-speed driving events and autocrosses, and I loved the accomplishment I gained on the race track. Future husband #1 was older by 12 years, successful in sales, drove a hot car, and being adored by an older man made me feel like a big deal. Despite some misgivings about tendencies that I saw but didn't give credence to, I accepted his marriage proposal on a beautiful seaside cliff in Hawaii. Shiny, sparkly, flashy, but controlling. I should have taken note.

Our life was full of adventures, many of them costly. We got started in business ownership via franchising when I was 29 or 30. My husband had gone to a franchise expo and came home with stars in his eyes. Meg, he said, people gotta eat, cars need to run, homes and businesses need to be cleaned. I didn't like any of those options. Then he told me about Great Clips, and that "it was as simple as turning on the lights and unlocking the door… everyone needs a haircut! BOOM, Meg, we'll be making lots of money!" If only it were that easy. He signed on, and we opened the first location about nine months later. Oh my, it was NOT simple or easy, and within six months, he was tired of the challenge and was ready to throw away the keys. We were losing money month over month, and the red line was much deeper than anyone projected. With a bit of sleuthing, I realized there was an internal theft problem. Because the husband was in denial, he didn't want to be the bad guy. What the heck? I didn't want to go broke! So I pulled on my Big Girl Pants, called the local police, and had the offending party, my salon manager, arrested in the salon in front of everybody. Talk about making a splash! The sudden impact of making a sweeping change made my staff so grateful. They knew she was a rotten apple, but no one told me that. Once she was out, the rest of the staff had a huge epiphany. I did care about them, and now they were ready to care about the business. My engagement with them to improve the culture was leading me to gain confidence, which my husband somehow resented. I think, looking back, what he really wanted was to be rid of the headaches of the business, but I was embracing my Inner Pit Bull. I was NOT going to give up without a fight.

SAY WHAAAAAAAAAAAAAAT?

The New Sheriff had suddenly arrived (that was me), and we were going to change directions. People buy a franchise in order to follow a proven system, execute a playbook, and win the game with known rules and scores. Just like the NBA or NFL, just like the military, if you follow what works, you will win. I stepped into the salon, worked with the staff to identify a new manager, and suddenly we were gaining stability and growth that my husband couldn't achieve. He simply didn't want to work that hard. We should all be saying this: Hello, owning a business is hard work. If you first take care of your employees, the money will follow. The stylists said, "what took so long?" and I agreed. The staff wanted a leader, someone who cared about them, their families, their paycheck. Fortunately, I was able to promote from within, and in short order one of my part-timers volunteered her expertise, stepping into the leadership role, and to her credit Gayle turned the whole place around.

Along with learning how to run a family haircare salon, I took on the role of Great Clips Chicago Co-Op President. I was voracious in wanting to learn how to run a profitable business. Since there were no other major metro markets to learn from, I created three different committees and invited other business owners to learn best practices. Little invisible Meg wasn't invisible any longer. I started to get recognition from the Regional, and ultimately the Corporate, staff. I learned from herding cats in my own salons, to now herding a bunch of disparate franchisees in the market to work together to create a strong bond and brand. Finally, we were all starting to realize profitability through implementing and executing the Great Clips business model. And in 2001, at the Great Clips National Conference, just days after 9/11, I was awarded the Co-Op President of The Year award.

I had won minor awards and recognition over the years, but this Co-Op President of The Year Award was BIG. Great Clips is very well known and an expansive nationwide system, but had only opened in B and C level markets like Milwaukee, Des Moines, Minneapolis, Denver, and Orlando. Chicago was their first foray into a major market, and because my husband was a pioneer, we were only the seventh location open in a huge, vast, competitive landscape. We struggled to compete in the value-priced family segment. But consistent application of the system and some smoothing of my competitive franchise owners' egos enabled us to cohesively move the needle of market share and open a lot more salons. We built trust with the stylists and customers by providing a great work environment and attention to detail, and once the repeat customers became committed customers, the realized profitability allowed many of us to expand exponentially.

During the Great Clips years, there was another event that stretched my personal limits. My husband was increasingly upset by my successes, and he more frequently was saying that he wanted to be divorced; that being married, a dad, and a business owner were not who he wanted to be. Say whaaaaaaaaaaaaaaat? This franchise idea was his pie-in-the-sky, get-rich-quick dream. More than any other thing he wanted to walk away from, marriage was something he was not good at. So, he brought it up again on a "date" for what would have been our 10th anniversary. I'd heard it enough, and while he used that "I want a divorce" phrase as a control/fear mechanism, I wasn't afraid any longer. He was proving that he wasn't good at following through on ANYTHING. And like everyone who chases shiny things, he would make great pronouncements about how successful he was going to be, but now I had earned success without him. Suddenly the words came out of my mouth; I was done, I wasn't crying, I had called his bluff, and he was stunned.

Divorce was never in my plans, and I worked hard to be a good wife and business partner. I was definitely not invisible, but not quite fabulous. In the end, he bitterly said no way to child support or alimony, just the three salons that were open at the time and "good luck with that" on my way out of the mediator's office. My son, who was then seven and is now 31, was devastated. I am not a quitter, but there was nothing left to repair in this case. Eric needed a nurturing household, not a bitter one, and he actually became a better man by splitting his time with both parents. I was the business side of parenting. Getting toxicity out was cleansing, and my husband needed to go.

Striking, isn't it, that his dream(s) became my obligations to operate and manage because he was a quitter. He quit on me and the businesses. But, we all know that big growth opportunities emerge when you're the one left holding the bag. Just as it was uncertain and unstable for a time with the arrest of my former manager, it was the same with my husband bailing out, and I needed to scramble. Where to live, how much to pay myself... do or die decisions we single parents need to make to support our children.

My ex has proved to be a dreamer all these years, and my son has watched him struggle to grow. He was a great dad on the weekends but not much of an enforcer of homework or practice at sports and music. I was the Enforcer. One of the most poignant events of my life happened one night with my son after he graduated from college. We sat on the back porch sipping really good tequila, and my son volunteered this: "Mom, I didn't know you owned businesses, I thought you were just a single stay-at-home mom... you were there when I got on the bus, and home when I got off." That moment sticks with me as proof that, despite all of the upheaval and demands of single parenting and business ownership, Eric realized the benefit of a mother who focused attention on the important stuff, like being there and nurturing his education and curiosity. Work was work, but I was Mom when he was home from school.

Just about two years after his dad and I finalized the divorce, Eric and I had some fun surprises to navigate. One was a 7 figure cash on the barrelhead offer to sell my Great Clips salons, and a contract to stay on for three months. I was delighted and celebrated with Eric in a big way. I knew his dad was jealous, but he was the one who didn't believe, and I did. His dad couldn't believe the size of the exit, and I could. Eric witnessed the fighter in me, and that's why his comments will forever linger with me. I wasn't "just" a stay-at-home single mom. He witnessed a strong, confident woman.

Another surprise came around that same time, around

2002. The former VP of Franchise Development at Great Clips started a new consultancy group. He was hand-picking the first founding members and tapped on my shoulder. Jeff Elgin's vision was to accumulate the Best of The Best in franchising, representing great business concepts while offering franchise industry expertise at no fee to the interested party. The company's founder called me at the time, saying that once I was completely done with my Great Clips transaction, I might want to consider using my Psychology degree and all those years developing the Chicago Great Clips Co-Op to help other people realize their dream of franchise ownership.

ABSOLUTELY. What a perfect marriage of my skills, ability to work independently, and mentoring mindset to help others become their best financial version of themselves.

When I joined FranChoice, I had no husband, no income, no other financial safety net. It had been years since I had a boss other than myself, so why not try my hand at something risky and rewarding? I had successfully sold my businesses, but that 7-figure sum is not what remained in my bank account after taxes. As I experienced the first time, being a single parent is very motivating. Being 100% commission is equally motivating. Since my first job at Banner Personnel, everything I did turned into financial success, so I confidently went forward. I'd never been a consultant before, but I was willing to learn. Besides, being self-employed meant I controlled my destiny, the hours I worked, and the income potential was unlimited. I am competitive, and I wanted to show my son that I was disciplined as his Single Mom to make our household financially stable. Driven and determined was sometimes construed as being aggressive and bitchy, but I turned a blind eye to that nonsense. I wanted Eric to learn to enjoy the fruits of my labor, so I ditched the guilt trips so many of us impose on ourselves and spent money on activities we could do together. I'm not talking First Class, but I was investing in meaningful experiences for us, Mother and Son.

My consulting work takes a ton of hard work to generate leads, much less a paycheck, but I was making great strides at the end of the first year. I was also getting a little restless in the personal department and started dating again. In 2002, I met my second husband, who was the CEO of a franchise company in our portfolio. It felt like a fairy tale to meet and marry my Knight In Shining Armor. He wined and dined both me and my son, he spent like everything needed to be First Class, and we thought we won the lottery. After getting married in 2005, he bought me a whole new wardrobe, new shoes, told me how he wanted me to dress when I was on his arm. Together, as husband and wife, we were The Power Couple of the franchise community. We were like the captain of the football team and the head cheerleader. The problem was he was a philanderer. After five years together, he one day announced… "I don't love you, I don't like you, and I don't want to be married for one more day."

This devastating blow came in April of 2008, just as the Great Recession started. In the blink of an eye, I lost a husband, three step-children, a role model in business for my son, and I lost the role of Co-Owner of that franchise business. In short order, I can't even begin to convey the total devastation that followed. Emotionally, financially, and physically, I was THIS CLOSE to bankruptcy, What a failure. I had been the Fairy Tale Queen of the Franchise World, and suddenly everyone knew that I had been unceremoniously dumped. Even more devastating was what I learned from our friends, who reported that I had been IMMEDIATELY replaced by a new Queen. She moved into our home the minute I was escorted out. Literally, she was being shown around town on his arm the very next day. Jaws were dropping, and he didn't care. He had his new girl.

See a pattern? Ugh, it is so obvious to me now. Those were two husbands who like shiny, sparkly, exciting things and give up on the hard work.

After being on top of the world, how does one rebuild from that? I wondered the same thing. How was I going to lick this recession and earn a living? It took months of soul searching, tears, and counseling for both my son and me. How would we pay for college? How would I rebuild my career in franchising, and keep my chin up while still having to see the a$$&*!+ at industry events (and he brings her, too)? Well, it was another lesson, ladies, in sucking it up, showing it off, and faking it until I made it back. And I did! I walked up to the stage at the FranChoice conference to take my place as a Top Performer in 2012. It wasn't fast or easy, but in 4 years, I was back on top and making great money once again. Indeed, in front of the jerk, I was also recognized by my peers and franchise colleagues as a winner and quickly got the nickname The

Franchise Fashionista. I have always had a great sense of style. Take that, ex-husband.

IT'S LIFE ON MY TERMS

Now, there was a paradigm shift taking place. Confidence had crept back into my aura, and I finally believed that I deserved the accolades and attention. I am proud of the fact that I balanced many roles and responsibilities during those years that I was a single parent, and certainly one of my greatest successes is raising a boy to become a self-sufficient, confident, professionally accomplished man. Today, he lives next door to me in a farmhouse adjacent to my office. I am not a helicopter mom and never was. We can go for weeks without seeing each other or having a meaningful conversation, but we know we have each other's backs. When Eric's appendix ruptured the first month of his freshman year of college, he had to pull himself together. It was 2008, and if you remember the start of that terrible year, aside from my unforeseen divorce #2, everyone was stressed about jobs, income, mortgage payments, and other bills. He was forced to drop one class and got a D in another, but my son graduated on time... with honors four years later. Confidence and a blind eye to failure are two traits he credits me with instilling in him.

To this day, literally last weekend, Eric talked about those two men and marriages, and he shakes his head about the dreamers and schemers, losers of love and money. As he plans his wedding next year, he also knows he can count on me for financial guidance.

If we fast forward in time, here is what happened over the years that followed The Great Recession and Divorce #2.

2012: I was walking the dog around the block one afternoon late in the summertime, and something made me stop dead in my tracks. It's like the hand of God came out of the sky and held my shoulders, planting my feet firmly in place. In that moment, I realized I had enough money in the bank to pay off my mortgage and the other half of my son's college tuition that his dad reneged on. In four short years, I went from total devastation to financial freedom. From that day on, I have viewed every day as another day of retirement. I work when I want to work, and I play when I'm done. I never beg for business, and I don't chase. It's life on my terms, and I can confidently tell you that Confidence became my middle name.

2013: The worst health scare of my life started in January with a persistent cough. By March, I couldn't walk the length of a room without running out of air. People commented that my skin looked ashen. During that year, I was unable to work for about nine months with something that behaved very much like COVID does but was a fungal infection in my lungs and sinuses. September brought some relief via surgery, but I had no income during most of that year. Thankfully I had paid off my mortgage in 2012 when the money was there, and I still had savings. Learning financial lessons via business ownership taught me to take care of my obligations and make hay while the sun was shining. I was back on the map by the beginning of the new year.

2014: I had signed up for It's Just Lunch, a dating service. I had been single long enough, my kid was living on his own, so I was ready to feel my hormones again. In February, I was set up on a date that was NOT lunch, was at a cheesy bar, with a man who could barely walk and didn't look like "my type." It was rainy/snowy that night, and my workday had been horrible. I arrived late and immediately my date was not impressed. It was going to be another dud of a date. But we connected in the last few minutes we were together at the table, when I confessed why my day had been so bad and why I was not engaged. As I scrolled through my pictures to show him some winter damage in my home, I came across my fully-stocked wine cellar and collection. Pete asked me about my wine preferences and suddenly, we had another date. A total turn-around from the first one, we both arrived early and met on the steps of the Art Institute, had lunch overlooking Millenium Park, drinking a great bottle of French White Burgundy. Well, it was just perfect. The rest is history...

2015 was a whirlwind of recovery and discovery. Pete broke his collarbone the prior spring, and by mid-year of 2014, had a full hip replacement. So with those major surgeries, let's just call 2015 the year of "getting to know you," as we traveled to around the US and Europe, and back and forth between IL and WI, for both work and fun. Pete had long owned a 230-acre property in Milton, WI, and we went up to the farm weekly to play Country Mouse. He also had a small house on the lake, facing west for daily sunset watching. I have long been an outdoors lover, and we had a blast taking down trees with our chainsaws, removing invasive species of trees and plants, winter snow activities galore, and summer fishing, kayaking, and paddleboarding. He knew I was The One. But it took me a little longer.

2016: My BEST FINANCIAL YEAR EVER. My franchise consulting business was like a freight train of momentum, but it didn't dominate my time. My personal life was fulfilling, Pete and I were traveling extensively, and life was in balance. So many men had initially told me that they love being with a strong, financially secure woman who won't suck them dry. But during my years on the dating scene, many of those men ran away when they realized how strong I was and that I did not need them. I wanted to be with them and be an equal. They loved the idea of me but were petrified by the reality of me. I should have realized how weak and insecure those men really were, and yet I was now living with a man who was walking the walk, not just talking the talk. Emotionally supported and financially secure, life was grand, and I was on top of the world again!

2017: After three years of living together, and living a glorious weekly blend of city mouse/country mouse activities, Pete and I were driving back from the little lake house in Wisconsin to life in the suburbs of Chicago. We had long been talking about Us, Our Life, what WE wanted to accomplish. I had long been waiting for him to Pop The Question. Pete turned to me somewhere near Rockford and said, "Look, I'm ready. But I don't want you to feel pressured, so when you're ready, just ask me." Like whiplash turning my head towards him, I looked at him quizzically and asked, "Just to be clear, what am I asking you?" He replied, "Well, since our first date, the one thing we both wanted but haven't done is to be successfully married to the right person. You're the one, but I don't want you to feel pressured. When you're ready, just ask me." I said, inside my head, IS THIS WHAT'S TAKING SO LONG? HE'S WAITING FOR **me**? At that moment, I turned to him and asked him. It would have been rude to make him wait any longer to marry me. Two weeks later, in front of my parents, son, and best friend, Pete and I were married by his best friend, the pastor of our church. No pomp and circumstance, no rings or flowers, just a perfect 11-minute ceremony in front of God and a few loved ones. My country farmer & Wall Street finance guy quietly married his forever wife, the Franchise Fashionista & Chainsaw Mama. FINALLY!

2018 and current: We sold our homes in Illinois in order to spend more time in Wisconsin. I will always work primarily in franchise business development, but I have learned so much more about the environment through our Tallgrass Wetland and Prairie Restoration business. Pete and I share the love of entrepreneurial activity and have been blessed to be sought after for mentoring and coaching small business owners to achieve greater success. While I now live and work amongst the prairie, we keep a small apartment in the Chicago area to stay close to family and friends. In the world of abundance, I hit the jackpot. Pete and I are partners in a few businesses that he owned prior to meeting me, and we employ a diverse group of people across a few states. Some are outdoorsmen, some are financial whiz-bangs, and every day brings a new opportunity to learn something new.

COVID brought some unexpected rewards. When the whole world shut down in March of 2020, I did what everyone else did... I put on my Pilates pants and never seemed to change out of that wardrobe. By about May, I was DEPRESSED. There was nowhere to go and no place to show off my Franchise Fashionista attire! Pete came to the rescue with a brilliant idea: build a new building for our Tallgrass employees, and take over the office they had outgrown. With a little paint, new flooring, and lights, I had somewhere to go! My office overlooks those 230 acres of prairie and wetlands; my art collection surrounds me; I have a Black Lab for a walking partner and a husband who works in the office downstairs. Believe me when I tell you that the Best Thing Ever is a husband who comes up to visit with me, looks me up and down with a grin on his face, and he flirts with me. The Fashionista is happy once again!

When I reread this chapter and think about the crazy stories that didn't make it into writing, I am awed by the resilience I never believed I could have developed back when I was an anorexic. The last few years have been both amazingly rewarding and challenging, but there isn't a day that goes by that I take it for granted. I've been blessed to elevate my visibility and experience in business, and be sought after for speaking engagements to share my knowledge and expertise.

I'm not invisible and never will be again. I am rich in so many ways and still building wealth in many diverse and wonderful ways. My mother says I focus too much on money. That's not really true. When you have money, that solves the money problem. When you have wealth and an abundance mentality, you can use it for good, for the betterment of others' lives. But always, put yourself first. Becoming turns into being.

Go on, be FABULOUS!

ACKNOWLEDGMENTS

Dorris Burch, for her love and support; Photos by Stacy Kaat, Milwaukee; Social Media and Brand Management by Tamara Burkett (behind the scenes queen); Peter Layton for unending love and belief in strong women; God and The Universe for lifting me to new heights I couldn't see myself.

ABOUT AUTHOR

As a Student of Humanity, Meg Schmitz' mission has been to help everyone recognize hidden talents and tap into the confidence to Take The Leap into new endeavors. Writing has been a life-long passion, and Meg knows that story-telling is the connector that brings all of us together on this journey of life.

ABOUT MY BUSINESS

Meg is a decades long independent franchise consultant, following 11 years as multi-unit franchisee with Great Clips. A diversified business owner, employer, consultant, board member, and angel investor, Meg and her husband are ardent supporters of the environment, mentors to entrepreneurs, and serial networkers.

Website
https://www.megschmitz.com

Facebook Personal Page
https://www.facebook.com/meg.schmitz1

Twitter
@Guru_Franchise

Instagram
schmitzmeg

THANK YOU!

Thank you for reading my story – if I can support you in any way or if you just fancy connecting – I'd love to hear from you!

Jeannette
Gaiter

OUT OF THE SHADOWS

The stately sunflower has a curious secret. It is a late bloomer. Like the sunflower, I too am a late bloomer. Recently I had the opportunity to run for public office, become an inspirational speaker and a published author. Want to know another secret? My life was not always like this. As a matter of fact, when I was 8, I embarked on a 54-year journey of invisibility and living in the shadows. As you listen to my story, which is one of epiphanies and choices, I invite you to relate to it, find nuggets of truth from your own story and let those nuggets speak to your heart.

"Jeannette, I need your help right now!" I looked up through sleep laden eyeballs to see my father leaning over my bed, tears running down his face. My little 8-year-old heart was pounding like a jackhammer because I had NEVER seen my father cry before. As I crawled out of my bed, I wondered what was happening until he said to me, "Your mother has locked herself in the bathroom and is trying to kill herself. See if you can talk to her." I suddenly knew this was my fault and I needed to fix it! I would promise to be perfect and not make her mad. So, promise I did. The sun, the moon, the stars. Anything that would make her come out of that bathroom. I was eight years old, panicking, and about to be motherless.

Thankfully, after minutes of pleading, a tear-streaked face and hunched shoulders that screamed defeat emerged. She was alive! Life could go back to "normal"! Or could it? Unfortunately, life did not go back to "normal." I had made perfectionistic promises that my eight-year-old conscience was struggling to keep. To secure my mother's stability, my life underwent major pruning, and the era of "Mothertending" began. I watched her like a hawk, noticed anything I did that upset her and worked tirelessly to not repeat those actions. I was a square peg whose corners were painfully shaved off day after day. I did not think about who I wanted to be when I grew up. I thought about who I needed to be to keep my mother stable.

Life threw me a challenge that day that I was not prepared to deal with. When this occurs, we look for ways to cope with the problem because we do not have the skills or ability to solve it. Unfortunately, although those coping mechanisms help us to deal with the challenge at that time, they can affect our lives negatively for many years after the challenge is gone. The coping mechanism I chose that fateful day followed me, like a silent panther, into my 60s. Can you relate?

My "Mothertending" continued, and over the next ten years I became an invisible, shadow-living expert. That was my seed's superpower! No beauty, no blooming, just waiting longingly for water and warm delightful sunlight to help it grow, but I refused to allow my seed to grow! I kept it buried under dirt and gravel for over a decade!

Hey! Put out that seed lamp! I need total darkness here to be invisible! My seed just could not catch a break! My invisibility was a requirement for my mother's happiness which kept her alive! Covert operations over the years began with school activities and overachievement in my schoolwork. School was a safe haven for me. It counteracted the darkness that I experienced around my mother.

At 14, I got my first job! With all my newfound money, I considered moving out of the house at 15. My mother's mental illness and my hormones were like gasoline and matches. After figuring out my expenses, I fell short by $50.00 per month! No!!! I hunkered down, began saving for college, and got even more busy in high school on sports teams to avoid my tense home situation. I graduated, in 1977, 12th in a class of 500 students. I had figured out how to cope. Or so I thought. Looking back, my relationship with my mother was anemic at best. I was just running from that huge self-imposed responsibility that I could not shoulder. I was protecting myself as much or more than I was protecting her. I think both my mother and I resented my "Mothertending." It widened the chasm between us until the day she passed away.

My running eventually took me to college to escape my confusing home environment. Hours of sleepless nights and tension-filled days were spent making the choice to go to college. I was in the business of keeping my mother happy and her rants about my leaving grated on me like fingernails on a chalkboard. No happiness here! For the first time, I put on my big girl pants, stood up and fought for MY dream to save the world by finding a cure for cancer. Two years into my major, sitting by myself and repeatedly filling test tubes with the same bacteria, I realized that I could not tolerate the solitary, repetitive work environment. I chose instead to major in social work with a teacher's certificate on the side.

MAKING CHOICES THAT ALLOWED ME TO GROW

I began making choices that supported my need to have human connection. These choices allowed me to grow and be more visible for the first time in a decade. Blessed, blessed people! Even if we are introverts, we all need OUR people, our tribe. They love us unconditionally, they want the best for us, and they believe in us even when we don't believe in ourselves. Who are your people? I met some of my tribe, who became my spiritual mentors, when I made a serious commitment to God in 1980. He became my center and my reason for living. He was the most important person in my tribe. I recognized that God was a person to have a relationship with, not a religion. This was an epiphany for me! I learned so much about who he was, how he operated and his great love and mercy for me. I smiled broadly as I saw God work in my life and in the lives of others back then and I still smile today! Although I did not fully bloom at this point, it was the time of my life when my plant did some serious growing. My tribe provided warm delightful sunlight and water for my parched and barren soul. My seed finally broke through the crusty soil and had a stem and even some leaves. I was on my way to blooming!

Regrettably, that growth was short lived. In 1981 I married my best friend, Lew. He was a larger-than-life kind of guy with enormous charisma and an intense love for God. We had a small intimate wedding, attended by our best friends. My parents were conspicuously missing. I was not marrying a nice white Catholic and I was leaving the church. That was more abominable than going to college. This choice honored me and my relationship with God, instead of being who my parents wanted me to be. I was content with my choice. However, choices have consequences! My parents disowned me, and I did not see them for almost three years!

I began to realize that I was going to have some challenges a few years in my marriage. Lew had a powerful, magnetic personality. He was a wonderful man who loved God, his family, his friends, and his community. People had a great deal of respect for him and were just naturally drawn to him. With his powerful personality and my previous history with my mother, it became cushy and comfortable for me to retreat into those familiar shadows once more and allow my husband to take the limelight. As I skillfully executed my superpower of invisibility, I was also challenged by my own rigid beliefs about the role of a wife. I believed I could not have my own opinions! My husband had the final say and that was that! This intensified my invisibility and put a major strain on my husband. It is impossible for someone to never have opinions. I reacted with harsh biting words and meanness. Another epiphany for me was that God created me to be unique. I began to speak up and make decisions that supported me. This change, hard for both of us at first, made our marriage much better. The humongous load lifted from my husband's weary back, and I began growing again.

All this while the background music of my life was my deeply entrenched "rut." When my father passed away, my mother moved to Fort Collins to be close to me. I quip that God has a great sense of humor. Every mother wants to have the daughter she despises take care of her, right? It was certainly a journey! From 2001-2015 I did active "Mothertending" as my mother's health declined. Out came the old coping skills to deal with her. I fit in the best I could and just dealt with the outcome when I could not. I also tried to resolve some of the issues with my mother. During the last few months of her life, we were finally able to make some strides toward a fairly normal relationship. For this, I am very thankful. I am also happy to say that the last years of my marriage were exceptionally good as we stepped joyfully out of legalism and just loved each other.

Life's seasons changed and so did those closest to me. In 2015 I said good-bye to my mother and also to my 49-year habit of "Mothertending." After her death, I made momentary dashes out of the shadows to take care of myself, only to remember I still had other people to take care of! I didn't have time to grow my own garden. Or maybe I was scared. Have you ever avoided doing something because you were scared you would not succeed? More changes came along as my youngest child moved out of the house in 2018, and my husband passed away in September of that same year. I had no more lives to support. I was left with me. Just me. That barely growing plant was standing there in the middle of the field all by itself. This was terrifying and I stayed very busy by starting a business.

STAY OUT OF THE RUT

As COVID hit, I was forced to stop as my business ground to a halt. As I sat on my comfy living room loveseat one day, God began to show me a panorama of my 54-year shadow-living pattern that I created when I was 8. Another epiphany! He politely asked me if I would like to continue living in this way. My answer to that question was an emphatic NO! I desperately wanted to grow and bloom!

That statement began my enlightening journey out of the shadows. It required choices and changes. It took serious resolve and persistence. In order to climb out of my deeply entrenched rut, it required seeing my own brokenness and self-betrayal. Do they make a rut elevator? That sure would have been easier! With a torchlight in hand, I explored the dreams I had slammed into the closet.

My wonderful therapist helped me stay out of the rut and became a part of my tribe. She brought to light a lie I had been telling myself for years. I frequently stated that I did not know who I was. Her response was, "I think you do know who you are. You just told me who you are." This gave me a moment's pause. Why would I tell myself that

I did not know who I was when I did? Back to God for answers! Another mystery solved. It was less painful to tell myself that I did not know who I was than it was to admit that I had betrayed who I was for most of 54 years. As God told me this, I knew immediately that this was the truth. Accepting this truth was difficult and incredibly freeing.

I realized in 2021 that I wanted to be an inspirational speaker. My life was too hectic and busy with the business to accommodate that. My business partner needed to know what I was thinking. I had a great chat with her, and I stepped back. The next day I booked my first speaking engagement! Within two months, I had booked 11 speaking engagements. I spent less time on the business and held space for speaking and sharing this story. New things cannot grow and bloom if there is no room. Talk about an epiphany!

As I look back and reflect on my 54-year journey, here are a few of my revelations:

1. We need to step into that warm, delightful sunlight and allow ourselves to be seen. Being invisible, its overrated. We will always grow when we stop fitting in and become our authentic selves.

2. We need our tribe to water us and help us sort out our tangled webs.

3. We need to choose to nourish ourselves. I spent years waiting for others to nourish me, but they seldom did. I learned I need to do that for myself.

4. Fourth, to step out of the shadows, I needed to do three things:

a. Listen –. If you are too busy to see or hear where you need to change, then you will never make it out of the shadows. Ask me; I am a pro at that!!!

b. Choices – Once we listen, then we need to make intentional choices to get somewhere else. The more INTENTIONAL CHOICES we make the better. Our life will go in the direction we want it to go as we make more and more intentional choices.

c. Action- For choices to make a difference, we must take action. Make space for what is important. Without action, nothing happens.

I now make choices daily to step into that warm delightful sunlight and find my passions and my dreams. I do this by saying YES to new opportunities and challenges. The journey has not always been easy, but it has been so worth it! I don't have one moment of regret! I share my story with you to encourage you to emerge from your shadows, to dream big and to thrive! You can be a late bloomer like the strong and stately sunflower, but please do not be a never bloomer. Choose to bloom, now.

ACKNOWLEDGEMENTS

First and foremost I want to thank my heavenly Father for creating and loving me beyond anything I could imagine. I will be grateful for your love and direction for as long as I have breath. If it were not for you, I would not be writing this acknowledgement. I want to thank my husband (deceased) Lew Gaiter III and my children, Jon, Micah, Elijah, Josiah, Shama, Samuel, Lewis and Daniel. Being your wife and mother has forever impacted my life for the better. Thanks for your support as I have made some major changes! I love you so much and you bring me so much joy! Thanks to my friends Barry and Cari Wilson for being there before and after Lew died, and for encouraging me to find and be myself. You have seen me through the good the bad and the ugly for over 30 years! I will always appreciate your love and support! I want to thank my Noonshiner's Toastmasters group for listening to hours of speeches as I improved my story. You all are awesome and I appreciate you so much!! I want to thank all of my Polkadot Powerhouse sisters that have encouraged me in this journey! You are too numerous to list, but you know who you are! Thank you for being my tribe, and loving me just the way I am! Last, but not least, I want to thank Dorris Burch for her encouragement, editing and support as I have journeyed into this new area of my life. Thank you Dorris for your friendship and your help in getting this done!

ABOUT AUTHOR

Jeannette Gaiter is the mother of 9 children and Grandma J to 8 grandchildren. She spent 22 years home schooling her children and supported her husband through cancer and multiple political campaigns. She is co-owner of Boulder Raw, LLC and Jeannette Speaks is her platform for motivational/inspirational speaking. Her current presentation is "Out of the Shadows". She has spent much of 2021 speaking to women across the US. She will have "Out of the Shadows" published in 2021.

ABOUT MY BUSINESS

Jeannette Speaks is a motivational/inspirational speaking business. Jeannette desires to reach the hearts of her audience in order to encourage them to come "Out of the Shadows". She also desires to give other inspirational/ motivational presentations to help others be their best selves. You can learn more about her business at...

Website
JeannetteGaiter.com

Facebook Personal Page
https://www.facebook.com/Jeannette-Speaks-109271301550591

THANK YOU!

Free "Out of the Shadows" quiz to see where you might be in the shadows. Go to www.jeannettegaiter.com and click on Take Quiz.

Rachael
DellaCroce

FINDING MY FAITH AGAIN

I believe we are born whole. With our hearts full and with our minds clear. We are perfect. As we grow up, we experience loss and heartbreak. Our minds start getting cloudy. We no longer feel complete. We begin searching for things we believe will make us whole again. My story is one of many losses and many heartbreaks. A journey where choosing the wrong path would cause me to forget who I was and, most devastatingly, cause me to forget what I knew deep down would make me whole again.

When I was five, my parents got divorced. A family that was once whole was now broken. So my mom and the four of us kids moved into an apartment together. I was the youngest and the one that understood the least what was going on. We would see my dad on the weekends, and after church on Sundays we would go out for breakfast together. I have nothing but fond memories of that time.

My mom remarried when I was seven years old. She married a man who would become my best friend, my cheerleader, and one of my biggest supporters. He was everything my heart needed to remain whole. He was literally God sent for our family. My mom was very clear to him that he wouldn't have to parent us; she would handle that. So he could just be my best friend, and he was. They loved each other in the way everyone wants their parents to be in love. They were all I needed to see as a role model to believe that falling in love was possible. Growing up as the youngest definitely had its ups and downs, but he was always there for me. So overall, my days were full of joy.

My sister was nine years older than me, so to say I looked up to her was an understatement. I was like her baby doll when I was born. As I grew up, I became like all little sisters do and was more annoying than cute. She moved to California when I was 12 years old. We had shared a room most of my life, and now I would have my own room. Her leaving left me heartbroken. I started to show signs of OCD; I needed to protect myself from ever feeling this loss and loneliness again. I made sure nothing in my room would move or be lost. I knew where everything was, and I was determined to control everything. For the most part, I am still this way.

Luckily, she moved back when I was in high school. Her best friend at the time would include me in their outings. I was given back the sister I had lost for all those years. One night, she got in a really bad car accident at the bottom of our hill. I remember standing there alone, watching down the hill, terrified I could lose her again. It felt the same way it had when she moved to California, except I didn't know if I would ever see her again. She survived the crash, but she was severely injured.

When it was time for me to go to college, I wanted to go to an art school in Boston for photography. I remember visiting the school with my Mom, stepdad and sister. My sister didn't think I should move and felt it was too far from our family. My stepdad however, encouraged and pushed me to take a leap of faith. So I decided to go there. However, my sister was right. It was too far, and I only stayed for the first semester before moving back home.

Shortly after, my Mom, stepdad, and I moved to Philadelphia, only blocks away from the college I transferred to. Unfortunately, they divorced not long after. When he left, I felt like all the sun was being taken from my sky. When he left, so did my faith in God. I didn't know who I was anymore. My heart was severely broken, and my mind was dark and cloudy. I didn't feel like anything would ever make sense again.

Shortly after, I started pursuing a boy at my college. He wasn't the kind of guy I would have been looking for before, but I was no longer the person I used to be. I had made a promise to myself and God that I would wait until marriage to have sex. I believed that I was enough and plenty worthy for someone to wait until marriage for. I thought that if I met the right person, this would be worth the sacrifice in order to be with me. Unfortunately for him, this wasn't the case. Once I told him this, he ended the relationship with me. I took it as I wasn't enough, that I wasn't worthy of his love unless I could offer him sex.

ONE STEP FURTHER

I wanted to be with him so badly, and that I had lost him over this crushed me. I had to choose whether I could live without him or go against my faith. I decided to give him something I could never get back. I would have to give him something I planned to give only to one person. So I told myself he would be the person I would marry, which would make it ok. But what kind of person did I think I could marry that didn't think I was worthy of waiting for, and that I wasn't enough unless I could offer him sex? I should have been wise enough to see it then, but my first true love blinded me.

Everything after that decision was one step further and further from my faith. I lost God in my life, and I no longer felt worthy of his love now that I was acting against what he asked of me. So I moved in with my boyfriend and his roommate. The three of us got along really well. It wasn't that I was unhappy; I just wasn't me.

Everything that happened during the time with him was some of the most challenging and traumatizing things I have ever experienced. Our roommate committed suicide in the middle of the day in downtown Philadelphia by jumping off a parking garage. It messed with our hearts and heads so much. We didn't know how to get out of the darkness his death created. It made us feel like we needed each other to survive. I definitely thought I was the only positive thing in his life and wondered how he would survive without me.

We were together for three years and lived in three different apartments together. We weren't thriving in our relationship. We were surviving life together. After graduating from college, I decided I wanted more out of my life. He was my first love, so walking away from him would take strength I didn't think I had. I had become the person I thought he wanted me to be, so how would I ever figure out who I truly was? I was completely lost.

The loneliness of being alone was more difficult than I could have imagined. I didn't casually date anyone because I was so focused on finding my husband at that point. I would see the old boyfriend once in a while because the loneliness was suffocating. I was single for a few years until my now husband started working with me at a camera shop. Our first date, I offered him what I thought would show him I was worthy of his love. To my surprise, he didn't want that. Instead, he wanted to get to know me and take our time.

The beginning of our relationship was so much fun, and we just enjoyed getting to know each other. He reminded me a lot of my stepdad. He was fun and easy going. He treated people well and came from a good family. His parents were still married, and I remember feeling ashamed of my story. I never wanted to talk about my past because I assumed anyone hearing my story would believe I was too damaged to be with. I could always represent myself as if nothing that happened to me changed who I was. The truth was I was just being who I thought everyone wanted me to be. It would be a long time before I would be broken down enough to figure out who I indeed was again.

We dated for a year, and I broke it off before it got too serious. I just didn't know what I wanted or who I was. He asked me for a reason, and all I could tell him was it felt like the sky was yellow all of a sudden. I couldn't explain it, but it didn't feel right anymore. After a few months apart, I offered to pick him up from the airport, and I remember looking up at the sky that day and saying how blue the sky was. I realized I might have needed the time apart from him to realize he was the reason my sky was blue again.

A year after our breakup, which just happened to be New Year's Eve, I decided I didn't want to think of this day as the day I broke up with him. Instead, I decided to make it the day I proposed to him. His family was there, and so were our close friends. A couple of hours after ringing in the New Year, I had them play our song. After he realized they were playing our song, I got down on one knee and proposed to him with a ring. Ironically enough, only a few days prior, he had gotten me the most beautiful blue topaz ring for Christmas. His ring had the same blue topaz in it. We both had matching rings that night. It was meant to be. New Year's Eve is now our favorite holiday and is only remembered as the day we got engaged.

Five months later, we got married on May 22. I wore a vintage dress from the 50s, which was definitely my something old, and my topaz ring was my something blue. I had always dreamed of having my stepdad at my wedding; however, he didn't feel comfortable being around my family after the divorce. So I had my dad walk me down the aisle. I felt so loved that day, and it was full of so much joy. It was everything I had dreamed it would be and magical, to say the least.

After three years of being married, we decided to start our journey to parenthood. My husband and I knew this journey would not be easy. At age 14, my husband was diagnosed with Klinefelter Syndrome, making him most likely sterile. We knew we would most likely have to adopt. We started at a fertility clinic to see what our options were, and to our surprise we were able to do IVF alongside my husband having surgery to see if they could find any sperm. They were able to confirm during his surgery that he was indeed sterile. We almost had wished that we weren't given that hope because just like that, it was gone.

I BELIEVE IN MIRACLES

Despite our hearts being completely broken, we decided to move forward with the IVF cycle using a sperm donor. We had three beautiful embryos transferred; however the pregnancy never progressed past positive blood work. We continued on our journey through many difficult unsuccessful cycles. My husband felt like we should give up many times. Yet nothing made me feel like I could. I pushed forward with our fifth IUI, fourth sperm donor, and second fertility clinic, and it finally worked! The stars had finally aligned. We were past all the hardships, and now we could just enjoy this beautiful magnificent baby growing inside me.

Not far into the pregnancy, they saw an edema on the baby's neck. After blood work and an ultrasound with Maternal Fetal Medicine, we found out our baby girl had Turner Syndrome. This meant she was missing an X chromosome. Ironically the very reason my husband couldn't have a child of his own was because he had an extra X chromosome. They fit together like the most perfect chromosomal puzzle. He kept saying if only he could give her his extra X, then she might survive.

We named her Audrey after Audrey Hepburn. Audrey's quote—"I believe in being strong when everything seems to be going wrong. I believe that happy girls are the prettiest girls. I believe that tomorrow is another day and I believe in miracles"—was my mantra that our Audrey would survive the pregnancy. I honestly thought that the less than 5% survival rate meant there was a chance for a miracle. On our sixth wedding anniversary, we believe she passed away, changing what once was the most perfect day to one that would break our hearts forever. Through my healing journey, it has become the day that reminds us that she would have never been created without our marriage. She intentionally picked that day to remind us of our love for each other and for her.

Audrey was 16 weeks along at this time, and I had to decide if I wanted to be induced and give birth to her or be put under and never get to see or hold her. This was a week after we believed she passed away, yet my body hadn't gone into labor and didn't seem ready to let her go. So I chose what I felt I was capable of without ever knowing how much regret it would bring me. I just couldn't see how my head and heart would survive holding my lifeless daughter in my arms. No doubt I would have; I just couldn't see it at the time. So I never got to see or hold her. Her remains were buried by Share of Lancaster along with other babies that had passed away during that time.

After that, I couldn't be left with all this pain and my arms so painfully empty. This feeling of loss and loneliness was the exact thing I had been trying to protect myself from for all these years. Yet again, I was left alone, heartbroken, with no way to make sense of everything I had just experienced. I would now have to learn to live a life without her in it. A life I saw her in that was taken from me before it was ever given.

We tried two more rounds of IUI with the same sperm donor, and on the second, we ended up getting pregnant with twins. Ironically I wasn't on meds that would cause multiples, so this was a huge shock to the doctor. Yet, somehow this felt like our hardship was now being transformed with twice the blessings.

Only one of the babies was growing as it should. The one twin became a vanishing twin. Even though we got to see the heart beating at two different ultrasounds, it wasn't long until it stopped, and then the baby slowly began to vanish.

Years later, part of my healing was naming the twin we lost, Collette. We never found out the gender, however, I just simply asked for a sign as to what we should name the baby, and sure enough, I was given the name Collette. She deserved a beautiful name. It was the least I could do to keep her existence meaningful. We tried to stay focused on the healthy growing twin moving forward. It was so hard because anything to do with twins puts a pit in my stomach even to this day.

A week before our 16-week ultrasound, we went to see our favorite musician Patrick Watson. He was someone my husband discovered from Canada right after we got back together after the breakup. His music became a very important part of our relationship. We brought a onesie and black Sharpie marker to the concert that night. As soon as I got the chance, I ran over to him and asked him to sign it. I told him if in a week I find out I am having a boy, we are going to name him Watson after him. Before that night, I was really hoping it was a girl because I missed Audrey so much. After that night, though, it felt like we were going to get our Watson. So sure enough, a week later, we found out we were having our Watson.

I honestly thought the pregnancy was going to kill me. I felt like I was drowning the entire time. I would either lose my third child or die at any moment. For 37+ weeks, my only focus was keeping us both alive. I had both preeclampsia and gestational diabetes. I just wanted him to be out of what I felt was a lethal body and to deliver him safely and alive in my arms. The day he was born was better than a textbook induction. I even helped in delivering him after only a few pushes. Everything up until that point might have been extremely difficult; however the delivery was as smooth as possible.

Our journey was complete; my son and I survived. However, the trauma I continued to ignore from my journey to motherhood was going to find its way back into my head. My heart was holding all the pain from our losses, and it was too painful to think about and definitely too painful to talk about.

When my son turned 2, I decided to quit working full-time and savor all my time with him. My husband had been taking care of him full-time up until that point. But I needed that time with him now. I didn't fight so hard for him to then spend my days away from him.

A few months into being a full-time mom, I felt the

push to share my detailed journey to motherhood on Instagram. I was able to transfer everything in my heart to my head and into a series of videos. I felt such peace from this experience and I felt like if we could just talk about what we hide in our hearts and heads, we could truly begin to heal. My story felt safe in my heart, but it felt alive to let it out into the world.

I decided I wanted to continue sharing with others, but now I was ready to love and support others on their journey. I knew how hard it could be to start the challenging journey to motherhood. The number of women doing exactly the same thing was incredible to me. We shared our stories and were able to talk about our babies and journeys.

Faith and hope were what got me through my journey, and yet my faith wasn't tied to anything. It wasn't attached to God because he hadn't been in my life for so long. I could see the women with God in their life and the difference his love made for them. I thought if God could give them peace after what they had endured, then I, too, needed him back in my life. They were able to believe that they would hold their babies again one day in heaven and then for an eternity.

The last time I felt like myself was before I walked away from God. I could see parts of my old self in these women who were looking to God for everything. After talking with a dear friend, I decided to start going to church again. At first, I told my husband it was for our son. He will do anything for him, so he agreed that would be good for him too.

Our son had never been away from us outside of

family until that point, so leaving him with strangers at Sunday school was so hard for us. At this point, he was three, and we thought it would be just as hard for him. The woman that was with him the first day I later found out had a vanishing twin as well. She said when she saw Watson, she knew there was something special about him.

We continued to go to church every Sunday, and it was definitely the highlight of Watson's week. My husband and I finally had time to together since we never took the time to do that. After a month of going to church, my husband said to me in the car one day that all this good stuff was happening in our lives ever since we started going to church. He saw that God was the only difference. I was feeling it too.

God was working through us in ways I didn't think possible. We took a relationship course at church together, and it taught us so much about each other. As a mother, I have learned to do everything with love. All my son wants is to be loved just like God loves all his children.

It's two years later, and I can't even begin to explain the difference God has made in our lives. I am now running a Journey to Motherhood Group at my church, helping women lean into God during their own journey. I can tell them how he is blessing my family in ways I never thought we would be worthy of.

One Sunday, the pastor was talking about heaven, and he said, "some of you will get to hold your babies for the first time." It hit me that the day I was given the option to hold Audrey wasn't the only chance that I would regret not taking. The first time I hold Audrey and Collette, they will be living out their existence with me in heaven.

God is my strength. He never promised we wouldn't experience hardships. He did promise he would never leave us, and he will always bless us in more ways than we can imagine. He is my guarantee that I will never be alone and that he will take good care of my girls in heaven until I get there.

I can now see that a life with God is the only way to keep my heart whole and my mind clear. I know I will continue to experience loss in my life. However, I don't have to do it alone anymore. I can finally be me again. I am worthy of love. I am worthy of happiness. I am worthy of heaven and the eternity of spending it with all three of my precious children.

ACKNOWLEDGMENTS

To Audrey, Collette, and Watson, who have given me the greatest gift of motherhood.

ABOUT AUTHOR

I am an infertility and loss Mama. I have a degree in photography. My husband and I own a camera shop in Reading. We live in downtown Lititz which feels exactly like living in a Hallmark movie. At this stage of my life, I am focused on my growth and healing. I trust God has big plans for me and my family. I am committed to loving and supporting others.

ABOUT MY BUSINESS

Providing love and support to women experiencing infertility and/or loss on their journey to motherhood.

Website
linktr.ee/thefriedegg

THANK YOU!

Barbara
Gauthier

WIND THERAPY

When I was little, I wanted to fly. I believed if I could run fast enough, have enough wind beneath my arms or jump high enough I would take flight. I dreamed all the time I could fly, whether like a bird or like superman, I was flying. As I started to ride bicycles, I got some of that flight feeling from going fast down a hill and I loved catching air as I jumped off curbs and ramps.

My first motorcycle ride was part of a birthday present from a family friend when I turned 8 years old. The wind was magical, and I was hooked! The next summer, my opportunity to ride on the back of a motorcycle with a neighbor was cut short when my brother, who got the first turn, was met with misjudgment and got thrown off the bike and wrapped in barbed wire making my mom put her foot down that motorcycles were too dangerous, and I would never ride on one with her permission. So, growing into my teen years, I road without her permission. I found any and every opportunity to jump on the back of a motorcycle and get that near feeling of flying. When I turned 21, one of those rebellious rides showed me just how hard my guardian Angel was working to keep me safe, and I decided to give up the pursuit of 'any ride I could get' and stay on the ground. College, life, and family responsibilities all quickly piled on that childhood desire and buried the dream of flight and riding a motorcycle very deep and away from any hope of surfacing.

Fast forward 30 or so years to the beginning of 2020, at 54, my life has been churned up with unexpected changes. I find myself single and wanting to date again. Feeling guided to a particular site, I built a profile and started to meet up with men for coffee, seeing if there was any common interests or spark. One particular profile pic had a guy in a long-distance riding suit next to his motorcycle at the northern most part of the state. The little kid in me took notice that maybe here was a chance to have a ride that would be safe. The coffee went well but he was planning a trip the next week to go ride motorcycle in another, warmer state and time was not on my side. I had been given the 'I'll get back to you when I'm back in town' line before so I figured it would turn out the same. To my surprise and delight, a short notice dinner invitation squeezed in before the departure date and a stronger connection was made. I was able to see him off on his trip with his motorcycle, real thoughts and desires to ride forming in my mind.

As our local Minnesota weather warmed up to riding season, real talk about going for some rides developed. I'd need a helmet, and gear! Stuff I'd never thought of before when I was a kid, but absolutely necessary as a conscientious adult. This wasn't going to be just a ride around the block, I had a feeling this was going to become part of my life. A nice sunny April Saturday arrived, and we were off for my first ride. Although I had been very enthusiastic in our conversations, my driver was familiar with realities of a longer ride and didn't want to push my tolerance. We reached our destination an hour away and it felt like I had been on the bike for 10 min. More! I wanted more!! Three and a half hours later, he was getting tired and wrapped up our ride. I was hooked and ready to set another date!

Long distance riding requires one to build up their endurance to the bike and the weather, so intermixed with rides around town for fun were rides for miles. We did 350 miles around a lake, then a 500 mile run to get some donuts. It's always good to have a goal or destination on these longer rides. We then set our sights on a certified 1000 mile Saddle Sore ride in 24 hours. There is a wonderful crazy bunch of riders that do long distance rides in specific amounts of time and certify them with the Iron Butt Association. He's been doing these type of rides for years, but this was my first one and first one for him with a passenger.

In June, we left before dawn, sticking to the interstate as this was a distance ride, not a winding sightseeing ride. The weather was cool to begin but warmed up with the sun and that's why we were in layers. It was easy to converse or listen to music through our com system. It almost felt like riding in a car, but with all the windows down and your head out the window. I was loving every minute of it even if I had feelings of stiffness or achiness. We stopped at our destination for lunch and marveled how well I had done in not slowing us down during fuel stops. I'd made long distance trips with my family since I was a kid, so I knew how to get in and out to the car to not be left behind! This was a simple out and back trip along the same path so on the way back, knowing how much time we had left, we were able to do a little bit of 'drive by' sightseeing. We rolled in from our 1034 mile ride in just over 16 hours on the road. We were tired, but I was all smiles and ready to go again.

I CALLED HER BLACK BEAUTY

I was so hooked on this wonderful wind therapy, I wanted to go on a ride any good weather day after work. Unfortunately, my friend had other responsibilities and wasn't able to take me out all the times that I wanted to go. I was a bit frustrated and felt limited, but I also understood adult responsibilities. In our conversations, he said he could see me riding on my own in a year or 2. I want to ride NOW! Why wait? So, I hatched a plan to do that very thing. In spite of the 2020 covid restrictions and need for appointments to take tests and register for classes, I was determined to make it happen sooner rather than later!

When he found out I had my permit, he was supportive and started taking me around to the different motorcycle dealers in the Twin Cities so I could sit on different bikes and find the style that felt right for my height and skill level. The one I fell in love with was a

Kawasaki Z650, black with green highlights. I was so excited! It's considered a naked street bike without all the racy skins or windshield and fairings. I called her Black Beauty just like the story I loved as a kid. I couldn't wait to take my safety class the first weekend in Aug, get my endorsement and pick up my iron steed.

With his help, in the school parking lot near my house, I got familiar with my own bike. We worked for several days on basic maneuvers till I was comfortable on the neighborhood streets. To his surprise in a bold move on my part, on the 4th day, I road my bike 18 miles up to work on surface streets. I was terrified of traffic as I was still so new to the mechanics of my bike, but the fear was overpowered by the thrill of riding on my own. I became focused instead of fearful and I promised myself to ride every day I could so as to continue to improve my skills. On a new bike, I had RPM restrictions as I broke in the motor for the first 600 miles so puttering around town everyday was perfect for me.

My friend had also introduced me to the thrill of riding on a track and having advanced training with a group in our area called ZARS. I wanted to participate, but there was a minimum 1000 street miles needed before I could enroll in the beginner level and the season was fast coming to an end. I had spent a couple of weekends at the training track during the summer, watching and taking photos and talking with the other riders. They were having a member appreciation weekend the end of Sept and on Sat night it was decided to have one last level 1 track class. I had to be a part of it! How do I get 1000 street miles in a short amount of time? You guessed it, a long-distance ride!!

One could call me an enthusiast, or crazy, with my newly found passion to ride motorcycle in all its aspects. It seemed like I was trying to make up for lost time. I wanted to break in my bike, qualify to do a track training day and even do a LD ride all before I had to put my bike away for the season. My friend who had been riding for 40 years was trying to be the voice of reason and safety by way of experience, but I had such a bee in my bonnet as my dad would say, I had different plans.

Being a passenger and being a driver on a long-distance ride are 2 different things. I had to build up a different kind of endurance as well as figure out all the planning and preparation for documentation of the trip. Most long-distance rides can be done just about any day of the year, but there are several that are date specific, and the 4 seasons themed rides are some of those specifically dated rides. I had set my sights on the Fall Equinox, Sept 22, 2020. I didn't have much time to prepare, 6 weeks to be exact from the time I picked up my bike.

I WAS GOING TO SUCCEED NO MATTER WHAT

Once my bike could handle higher RPMs, I took to the freeways and often headed out of town on the weekends. One beautiful Saturday, I ended up in Moose Lake, MN. I had wanted to make it to Duluth and back but had to stop short to get back for work latter that day. I had my miles for breaking in the motor completed and scheduled an oil change and maintenance check. My bike was ready for the open road of a long-distance ride.

I downloaded the tracking software and worked with my friend to plan a ride down to Des Moines, leaving early in the morning and tracking my pit stops similar to what we did to get me ready for my first Saddle Sore with him as pilot. I figured if I felt good, I'd keep going to my true desire, a 1000 miles, and if not, I'd turn around and have a good 500 mile ride underneath me.

I could hardly sleep on the 21st, but I knew I would need every ounce of energy to make this ride. I had my friends and family cheering for me, but only a few knew what I really had planned and only one knew what I was really up against, and he didn't know the level of crazy I had committed myself to accomplish on my ride. In my mind I was doing a full Saddle Sore. No alternative existed.

My planning and preparation took flight at 4 o'clock in the morning at the neighborhood gas station when I got my first dated and timed gas receipt, turned on my tracking software, took a deep breath and hit the asphalt ribbon. The first couple hours were pure adrenalin. When the sun came up, I was in farm country. The golden hour was more spectacular than any other sunrise on the road I had experienced up to that point. The open road by yourself gives lots of time for thought and personal observations such as: skunks smell worse on a motorcycle; even little drops of rain hurt at 70 miles an hour; watch out for the potholes at the end of the new pavement; going between 2 semi-trucks creates quite a wind tunnel.

I had layered down to daytime clothes at an earlier stop so as I got into Des Moines, I was feeling pretty good, not too fatigued and knew I could go all the way to my planned destination. Carpe Diem baby! I kept heading south and working my planned fuel and food stops. I knew the key to success was keeping well hydrated and ahead of the hunger. I only had my backpack and a tank bag for my bike to carry food, clothes and supplies, so I made sure to take advantage of the convenience stores at the gas stations. Soon everyone watching my tracking knew I was taking the long road home.

I had created my own personal twist on the themed ride for the fall equinox. Since the sun and moon were sharing the sky equally, and I love stones, my planned destination was in Lawrence Kansas at the Summit Steps Minerals I had found a few years earlier to pick up a sunstone and moonstone. As I arrived on sight, I was surprised to see exactly 500 miles on my odometer for the trip. Yeah!! Unfortunately, the store was closed and available only by appointment due to Covid. BOO!! How could I have overlooked this potential snag? I walked back and forth in front of the store a couple times, stretching my legs and working on a solution. With nothing else to lose, I called the posted number to see what appointments might be available for today. After awkwardly explaining who I was, what I was doing and my specific need, Adam Guss, the owner of the shop, confided that he was actually in the back room, just having finished up the morning appointments and was getting ready to leave and was willing to give me a few minutes in the store. Heaven's tender mercy! On a normal day, I would have wondered around and looked at everything and left with much more than what I had intended, but the clock ticking on my ride was a friend to my bank account and I got in and out of there in record time with only 1 additional stone than the 2 I went in for.

Now it was time to refuel me and my steed and make the turnabout trip home. The adrenaline of success was waning as was the sun and I was a long way from home. I had sufficient time on the 24-hour clock so I planned a couple of side stops as the fatigue from riding in the full force of the wind without a shield was starting to set in. In Kansas City, MO I stopped for a few minutes at the LDS Temple where my oldest son was married. It was just off the freeway and gave me something to write home about. My next extended stop was in Des Moines at Krispy Kreme donuts. In my family, it's tradition to grab a box any time we go through town to bring home to the family. Hope they don't mind slightly squished ones as these are going in my backpack. I pulled out my layers for nighttime temps and was ready to make the long push to the finish line.

At 9 pm, 2 hours from home, I stopped to call home. Get the bathtub cleaned up, I said, and ready for a soaking bath with Epsom salts and essential oils, this body is gonna need it! I was more achy as time went on and with every stop, I could feel the rigors of the road setting in. As tired as I was getting, and yet so close to home, that only renewed my resolve that I was going to succeed no matter what.

The sparsely populated road gave me time to reflect on my adventures. This had been quite the undertaking to execute by a rider with only 6 weeks experience and I was very grateful everything had worked out as well as it had. I felt angels with me, guiding and supporting me. I knew family and friends were watching the tracking software and were excited I was almost finished. I even felt the traffic had been nice to me all day, almost like they understood I was on a mission. The weather had even cooperated with just a brief shower in the morning. The one thing that didn't seem to cooperate were the bugs! How many times had I washed my helmet?!

I pulled back into the same neighborhood gas station just over 19 hours and 1010 miles after I had left that morning. I grabbed my last dated and timed gas receipt and was ready to call it a day. There were no balloons, banners or cheering crowds to welcome me home, but the bath was ready for me, and I had a deep sense of accomplishment in my heart. I had done it! The next day, while recuperating from the battering of the wind on my body, I confidently registered for the track that coming weekend.

EXPANDING AND EXCELLING

Of all the motorcycle riders, there seems to be very few that cross over different riding styles. You have the cruisers, dirt bikes, street bikes and racing bikes. You have the LD riders and the track riders on the 2 extremes. Once you find your niche, only a few try and expand with other types of riding. I knew I was hooked on long-distance rides, but could I handle the different type of stress of the track? Luckily, my friend was a multi-passionate rider, and he was able to mentor me through both styles of riding.

ZARS has a fantastic program and leveled coaching to help new riders gain skills and confidence with mentors and classroom combined with live action on the track. As I was starting at level one, most of the focus was getting familiar with the track and best lines of travel to get through the variety of curves. I was understanding the physics of the lean and importance of looking where you want the bike to go. Every hour was broken up into 20 min segments; 20 min on the track, 20 min in class with the coach and 20 min to rehydrate and dewater. Every 20 min session out on the track brought new awareness and new abilities. The speeds were not very high, but the thrilling rush was real! Being in the evening session only afforded me 4 times on the track, but that's all I needed to know I wanted more! I realized I was eventually going to need 2 different bikes, one for my long-distance rides with bags and a windshield, and one for the track to play in the curves. As often quoted by experts in their fields, the right tool for the job.

Finding a passion I had buried all those years, I definitely didn't go home and put my bike away for the winter after that big week and weekend, I kept riding every day I could. We had freak snow in October that thankfully melted and then a warm November with lots of ride days. As I watched the weather into December, I started making plans for the Winter Solstice ride on Dec. 21st. As long as there was no ice on the roads and temps were in the 40's I was going to attempt to get another certificate. However, this newfound passion brought another unexpected blessing, a full-time job. I learned that Cycle Gear was opening a store in my area in December and were looking for all positions. I knew I had some great skills to offer, so I applied. In the interview I voiced my desired days off and all were granted. However, when the 21st arrived, we had just opened the store on the 18th and I just couldn't, in good conscience, leave for a day with so much work to be done. I did ride on the Solstice, but it was just to work and back. The next day, winter arrived with 8 inches of snow and Black Beauty was officially stabled for the winter.

I never pictured myself as one of the sexy biker girls dressed in skintight clothes laying suggestively over a Ninja bike, nor am I a tattoo laden Harley rider with leather fringe. And the beautiful thing I have found is there really are no stereotypical motorcycle riders. We all have our individual passion and purpose for riding. What I have found is an eclectic group of people that respect each other no matter their backgrounds and what they are riding because we all have a love of the open road and wind therapy.

For me, my time on the bike is 'me time'. Feeling one with my steed, moving through the air, sometimes slowly, sometimes at heightened speeds, time stands still. Hours pass like minutes. Wind therapy is clearing away the cobwebs of my thoughts, feeling empowered as the master of new skills, seeing the world through more appreciative eyes, touching a passion difficult to describe in words. I ride because I can.

But why now? At 54? When I asked God why He cared if I road motorcycles or not and why it was important for this dream to come forward now? He lovingly let me know He wanted me to have every desire of my heart, even the long-hidden ones, so I knew how much He cared about me and every dream and desire for happiness and joy. So, when I think the answer is 'no' to my prayers, it may actually be, 'not yet'. Wind therapy opens my ears to hear Him, in His time.

ACKNOWLEDGEMENTS

Thank you Dave Morton. Without you, this dream may never have become a reality. I'm grateful for my family and friends and all their support in what seemed like a crazy wild hair.

ABOUT AUTHOR

Barbara Giles Gauthier was born in Logan, UT, and had the privilege of living all over the United States as she was growing up. She currently resides in Minneapolis, MN. Her love of life comes through in whatever she may be doing. She has many interests and passions including crystals, essential oils, energy healing, and now motorcycles. Always a teacher, she will share her wealth of knowledge and experiences in a personal, heartwarming way. With her, family always comes first and if she knows your name, you are family.

ABOUT MY BUSINESS

Wise Owl Consulting combines multiple energy modalities to help individuals spread their wings and fly through the dark of night to become their best selves and learn to love 'who' they are.

Website
wiseowlcg.com

Facebook Personal Page
https://www.facebook.com/barbara.gauthier.3152

THANK YOU

I offer a free 30 min chakra balancing session using crystals. This is affective in person or through remote access. I also have a free 15 min rock consultation called, I got this rock, now what? For those that are new to crystal work and would like help identifying what a stone may be and what it can be used for and how best to care for it. Contact me through email or PM for access to my calendar for these and the whole range of services I offer.

Manoroma
Mimi

RISING OF THE PHOENIX: BREAKING CULTURAL SHACKLES

Throughout my entire childhood, I asked God, why? Why did you create me as a daughter and not a son? Well, now I understand why, and I am proud to be a girl/woman. The lessons I have learned in my journey (called life) are what made me who I am today.

My story is not very uncommon for daughters born in India. Until I said, "yes, I do" to my husband, I lived a life of chaos and was abused by my parents. I was always the victim of my dad's anger, followed with hours of beating, and to compliment the bruise, my mom would add on her personal issues in my body. A daughter in India can only be a burden for their parents and can bring loss for their family. You heard me right, LOSS. Parents are scared of dowry, yet dowry is the norm, yet the birth of a daughter is a burden.

Well, this is the society in which I was raised. On the contrary, it is very common to beat your daughter. Statistics (UNICEF report) only counts sexual violence and intimate partner/domestic violence but omits parental abuse or trauma in their reports. My story is of a neglected daughter of a rich businessman/father who wished for a son, the light bearer for his family.

I am braving to write my story, so many like me can stand up one day and say, "Enough is Enough." A girl is nobody's slave and an equal part created by the same God. She decides to join the family to share love and stand by their biased parents. By neglecting and hurting your daughters, you are questioning the divine order? How is that not punishable?

My poems come through channeling and healing techniques. With guided meditation and visualization, I am able to take myself to the event venue. I give my childhood self a voice to speak her feelings as I reach to the center of my heart and create my poems. You will find me revisiting my past, bringing the experiences and memories to the present, and weaving it all together. By letting my emotions flow, I heal myself. Once I have penned down my emotions, I read and share them. So let it begin...

RISING OF THE PHOENIX: BREAKING CULTURAL SHACKLES
BIRTH AND EXPECTATIONS:

The lights flickered constantly. It was a gray and stormy day in Bhubaneswar, Orissa (Currently known as - Odisha). My dad asked Solaria to hurry up and close all doors and windows. Loud thunder and darkness spread. Mother screamed, NOW. We have to leave now. Dad hesitated, but her water had broken. There was no help around. He immediately got his little moped out, nervous and excited, he drove her to the hospital.

After many hours of impatiently waiting, crushing multiple cigarette packs, he saw her older sister smiling and walking towards her. She hugged her excitedly and said, your firstborn is here, and she is beautiful. Many more packs of cigarettes and hours passed after when finally, my aunt demanded, "you coming to see your daughter or not"? His sunken face almost touched his chest as he walked unwilfully.

I looked at him,
With eyes soften.
He stared at me
As untouchable.

My mom streaming
For his feelings,
Felt lost
And unloved.

As he frowned,
And said,
Can't you bring me,
A son?

The heir to this family,
Who will hold me,
Until my last breath
And lit my pyres.

With watery eyes,
He turned his back,
The broken hearts
Of many.

A gentle hand,
Stopped him.
As he looked back,
He saw me smiling.

He picked me up
Tears rolling down,
He whispered,
I love you but
Wished you were my son.

His love for me grew over the years, and I have many pictures of him laughing and playing with me in the garden, holding and feeding me. In addition, to these pictures, my younger brother often teases him, "if you had fed me the same way you did for Didi (older sister), I wouldn't have been such a weak and sick child."

From our birth as daughters/girls, we are raised in judgment, feeling unwanted. As a wife, we are put into fulfilling not our but the expectations of others.

THE GARDEN OF HEAVEN WAS TAKEN AWAY FROM ME:

I would spend my entire day with my grandmother,

brother, and our maid (I will call her Solaria). I would chase and run after the butterflies and hop with the grasshoppers. Everything was so peaceful around the white-flowered tree situated right in the center of the garden. Rose, tulip, marigold, lilies, and sunflowers to name a few were planted by my parents. Then, I watched the family sit outside in the shade, sipping tea and munching on cookies while we were laughing and playing.

Bees, butterflies, dragonflies
Fluttering and flying everywhere.
Green grass and colorful flowers,
Grows with mesmerizing aroma
In this garden.

Cherishing memories,
Sun-bathing
I left my heart
In those ripe jackfruit trees.

I watched my grandmother
Sitting in the grass
I wonder, what she thinks
Staring at the dirt?

My brother and I,
run and hug her,
Hopping and skipping,
Now annoyed, she asks us to stop.
That we are bothering her too much.

Then she would
Pull us into her lap.
Tell stories of some,
Far away and unknown pasts.

I don't remember what age the new construction uprooted the entire garden with new office spaces and means to meet ends. My dad found business plans to grow his business and provide us with luxury. With that came many challenges and desires. I would watch the building grow above my heaven.

DARK UNANSWERED NIGHT

Why am I here, God? To cry every single day, to not be loved.

Do I deserve this pain for just being a girl?

Why did you bring me to this earth? Why God, Why?

Why do you not let them kill me? Why do you want me to go through the intolerable pain? Why?

Why did I not be their son? Is being a girl, a curse? Then why do you make me, God? Why?

Tears pouring my cheeks, wetting my nightgown. I wiped my tears and spread them on my forehead.

I sit straight and declare – my tears are not to be wasted. It will not be quiet. It will take all your happiness away. It will leave you in a forever drought that even pain will leave your side. The terror you will receive in your life will be an example of silent revenge.

I fall asleep. It's all I needed to write my anger down in my diary.

CLOUDS

The clouds circled again.
It's coming, I whispered in fear.

I saw his red eyes filled with anger.
He slowly walked towards me.
I cried before he even raised his hands on me.
I looked for my mom,
but she was a blind audience,
witnessing yet again,
her violent husband beating
an innocent soul.

I need you to protect me mom,
I spoke to myself,
but I knew she will never.
Not for me, at least.
Not for anyone, actually.

I begged her to protect me
when I was three, five, and seven
until I realized she has turned deaf.
Her heart nothing but frozen.

A stone hearted, evil
How can one deserve to be a mom?
Deserve to be loved.
She is a shame for all woman,
And the purity of mother.

THE DAY I COMMITTED SUICIDE:

I had it enough that day. Continuous hours of beating were enough to crush my soul and strength that I was holding for years of injustice, child abuse, and trauma. A promise is not mere words for me; it meant a bond through eternity. Well, I was fourteen then. Teen dreams and their world was always different.

Months before my finals, I was promised by my mom that once I finished my final paper of my high school examination, I could visit my aunt's house. She lived one house away from ours. I sowed many dreams in their garden, the flowers, free space to run around and relax away from the daily chaos—a chance to listen to my quiet mind.

She complained to my dad that I disobeyed her and left unsupervised, not waiting for my bodyguard, aka, my younger brother (four years younger than me). A call went to my aunt that Mimi is needed immediately, that she has to be present now. Four hours of beating came unto me with props that anyone can ever imagine. Hands, shoes, hangers, sticks, books, and utensils, to name a few. While I watched my mom stand saying nothing, half of my share was willfully taken by Solaria (the bravest queen).

I fought with my mind and tried to convince myself that suicide, of course, was not the only way out. I am strong and have handled pain for fourteen years. I can do this. As I heard, my mind burst into laughter, and asked, are you able to? I knew the answer. The next thing I remember, opening my eyes in the hospital ICU. I was carried by stretcher and whispers of nurses and doctors.

I did not die, I thought. Then why did I have to go through this experience? Well, sometimes, you must lose to gain yourself back. *"I lost a few months of my life laying in the bed of an old hospital and gained back my lost voice and courage."* Walking around the wards looking at the pain others are going through, I decided I will be there to help those who need it the most. Now, what should I do to help? I woke up to look at the newspaper. "If you want to become a lawyer, apply here." The door to my question opened. I knew what I would be in my life. *"Well, life brings changes; this is not the only thing you will become. Don't lose hope if you find yourself lost"*.

STOP, I YELLED. Stop, I yelled if you are a true son of your mother? If today anyone beats an innocent woman, it would be the last day they breathe on this Earth. The voice raised within me from nowhere. I found myself yelling at my dad and confronting his anger. My brother pulled my hand and begged me to stop. Raising my voice would mean hours of beating and witnessing violence. My brother loved me dearly, but I cannot let injustice succeed this time. The anger in my eyes made my dad stop immediately. He was in our bedroom to beat solaria. For she was peacefully sleeping and had done nothing to deserve such suffering. For the first time in my dad's life, somebody stopped him; somebody (a woman) was not scared by his anger. I saw fear in his eyes. I learned that he gets angry to hide his fear and weakness. As humans, we all hide our mistakes by our strength (positive and negative) and someone else's weakness. Once the false veil is lifted, one is vulnerable.

YOUR FEAR DOES NOT GO AWAY, YOU SIMPLY FIND WAYS TO OVERCOME IT:

I woke up early morning, tried fresh clothes suitable for a job interview. I knew I had to prove myself worthy. I was yelled at for thirty minutes by my mom for Rs.20/- to buy pain medication for my migraine. "I am no good; I do not understand the value of money, I am not worthy of earning, and I only spend, I am useless, I am a curse in their life, I am a burden," and on it went.

I could hear my heartthrob like a race car engine. Finally, I gathered all my courage and walked out of the house, determined. The whole drive, I was worried; what if this place was a scam or a means to force young girls into something disgusting.

I knocked at the closed door, and a shaky voice said, "may I come in." My interview started: I was asked many questions and finally aced it. I have a job now! My first job as a front desk/customer relation in an insurance company. The owner never hesitated to give the job to an entry-level college going student. His only concern was how I would manage my law degree studies and the job. It was a full-time position. You can start from Monday; his husky voice echoed my ears. I nodded and thanked him and his wife, whose smile heightened my confidence.

I waited for the weekend to get over soon. As I was about to step out of my house, my dad asked, where are you leaving in such a rush so early? The conversation I dreaded is here. I told him I had got a job and that I didn't have to ask anyone anymore for money. I proved my point in two days by getting a well-paid job. My dad was furious and said, 'daughters in our house, don't go out to work".

I said I am, and it's final. After many rounds of arguments and verifying the workplace and its owner's credentials through friends and other sources, he went quiet. I left for work – victory! Well, I learned you can never run away from problems; you face them with strength and standing by your ground.

More steps to climb and blocks to remove. We must go on. Don't stop if life is not always smooth.

Questioning may not always provide you with the answers you are looking for, but it can ignite thoughts of change in others. Traditions are built to follow, but the old turn into new ones as we evolve. Some of us fear to question others and our traditions. We, as women, are taught to accept what has been followed for ages. As a child, I struggled with figuring out the norms of society. With everything, I came up with counter-questions. I remembered my mom asking me to take a shower before touching the Aabir (powered colors used for Holi (festival of colors)). As always, I asked her why I needed to shower again, as I had already showered, and I was excited to play with the colors. She replied, you will apply the first color to the statue of God and Goddess, and then to your elders. Fair enough! God lives everywhere and in each of us. If God does not leave me when I am dirty or covered with mud, why should I have to take a shower? Well, as you can imagine, the conversation did not go well at all. I was grounded and wasn't allowed to touch or play with the colors that evening.

Another story, so in Bengalis, after marriage, women are supposed to wear a red and white bangle (symbolizing married woman). While men led a usual life as they did prior to their marriage without any traditional limitations. I refused to follow such traditions that will only bound women to define their relationship in life. I fought to look my usual self with many mental and emotional tortures by people around me. My mother-in-law every single day told me horrific stories about how it could affect my husband's life if I refused to wear those two bangles or tried to get a haircut in the first year of marriage. However, I did get the strength and support from my husband to keep fighting and following for what I believe in. I asked my mother-in-law about us not following the traditions all the reason for death in this world. Not knowing the reason behind the old traditions and fearing of bad luck can only cause damage to us.

Taking a shower before touching anything related to indoor keeps the germs away and cleanses all negative emotions we carry in with us. The white and red bangles are made of gemstones. As women did a lot of household chores (cooking, cleaning using their hands), the bangles constantly rubbing in the wrist activates the properties of gemstones and helps with blood circulation. But when did it get associated with my husband's life and death, and why should we be burdened with those responsibilities? Fear will never create followers; it will only create fearful, negative puppets. Learn the truth regarding your tradition; it has a beautiful story behind its creation.

FORGIVENESS IS THE BEST GIFT YOU CAN GIVE OTHERS AND YOURSELF

Ten to fifteen years forwards after the suicide incidence, I worked on myself and gained self-confidence, strength, and voice to speak up for myself and victims of the same cycle. But in 2016/2017, when my mom visited me in South Dakota and apologized, I felt a heaviness melt. A block from my heart lifted and disappeared. It did not take me seconds to forgive her for her doings. You see the guilt by the wrongdoers keep growing at a point where they cannot bear the pain. Whereas the sufferer grows stronger as their strength lies within them. They are no longer controlled and have broken free from the pain.

The stream flowed so gently today,
Staring at Lewis and Clark lake
Tears rolling down my cheek
I heard the rock shatter.

I felt lost,
Nothing to hold on to
Or against.
A gentle smile spread
In her face.

She hugged me,
I saw repent in her eyes.
She meant it
My heartbeat verified.

I smiled back,
Softly saying
It's okay.
Past is far gone,
Let's make our future
Bright.

Calmness spread through
My chest,
Butterflies surrounded
Where I sat.

Time to transform
From bitter to sweet.
Relations are meant for lessons,
To be learned from.

Not only the apology helped me heal, but it also helped me transform my thoughts around my emotions and relationships regarding her. Her story itself is painful, and I judged her for her doings, not knowing her side of the story. I do not defend her mistakes, but I have gone softer on my approach towards her. I listen to her more and try to be in her shoes when conversing with her. People may have their reasons to defend themselves for the pain they inflicted on others, but no one should suffer such pain.

Meditation, spiritual groups, writing, journaling, continuous learning, and sharing best ways to heal. In 2013, I learned I am pregnant. I found myself in an emotional rollercoaster. I can hold on to my past experiences or change the future. Two weeks before my ultrasound, I was gifted with a dream. I am a vivid dreamer, but this was different. I always wanted a daughter. I wanted to show my parents that a daughter is not a burden, and by giving her a good and loved life, I can prove how wrong they were. But that night, I was visited by two angels in my dream: an older male Angel and a baby boy Angel. The baby Angel asked me to hold his hand and walk with him to his home (sky). Instead, I asked him to hold my hand, walk with me, and stay with me. At that moment, I knew I am going to have a boy and not a girl. I woke up, and a thought immediately struck me – if I were to walk with that baby Angel I would have died, or my child would have died in my womb. So me asking him to join me in this earth life saved our lives. In the next two weeks, during my first ultrasound, it was confirmed that it's a boy.

As a child, I was told by Solaria, that I regularly sleepwalked. I would be seen chanting some kind of mantras in the worship room. All my experiences made me think that there has to be a power that we are not able to see in our earthly form. So, I started delving deep into it. In 2015 or early 2016, I tried an energy balancing session provided by a medium/healer/hypnotherapist. The session was about clearing once earthly and galactic karmic debts. Soon after that session, things changed for me. I met with my twin flame soul, and my heart chakra was activated. The meeting itself was so powerful and spiritual that my belief got stronger. There was nothing which could separate me from searching the higher Light energy/Source. My ascension had begun. Since then, until now, I have come to a point in my life where I am in a continuous process of transformation/ascension. While I heal myself in this process, I heal others in their journey and soul searching.

It took me twenty years to heal from my trauma and forgive my parents, and I am still in the journey. While I was going through the childhood abuse, my best friend was my "diary." I used to pour my heart out in these journals. I constantly worked on learning from my friends. I am gifted with great people around me. Few taught me to heal, some provided me with resources with my spiritual growth, and some stayed by me, holding my hand and lifting my spirit high. With everything I was blessed with, I had to go through my own and walk the journey of full recovery. I am still healing but now with the right tools. My faith and love are immense. I am now the light for many who are walking the same path. I shall carry on with my mission of love and Light. I do Intuitive Multidimensional Healing and Angelic Healing for those who are the warriors and want to have a trauma-free life.

Phoenix Rise
The ravens await her,
To touch the Sun, be destroyed.
For she felt the heat, burning herself down
Yet how she smiled,
Seeing her old self turn into ashes.

The childhood pains, norms,
Responsibilities and burden.
Shredding all, as her skin
Disappearing into flakes.

Kra! Kra! The hoarse sound of the raven,
She touched herself with new fondness.
Awakened, she flew like a hawk,
As she watched others suffer.

Calmly she spoke, let it go!
Of thy old self – let your soul help you rise,
Burn not your body but your habits
Chain not your mind but that what restricts it to fly.

Freedom will be found.
Awaken! Rise and Enlighten.

ACKNOWLEDGEMENTS

I am very grateful for the opportunity to be part of the awesome and multitalented Fab Factor – "The Fabulous Dorris Burch". You gave me the chance to be a published author. Your energy and talents are above and beyond all praise. I would like to thank from deep within my heart my husband Manas and son Ryan for their love and confidence in me who go through the benefits and tolls of my journey every day. For being so kind, understanding and patient. My parents and the lessons I gained. Without those experiences, I wouldn't be who I am today. Lastly, Divine Love and Light whose presence fill my heart with infinite love and gratitude.

ABOUT AUTHOR

Born in the East (India), Pallavee Mimi Das uses her paternal grandmother's first name (Manoroma) who she believes to be her guardian spirit soul. Manorama Mimi is a Poet, holistic coach, mentor, teacher, energy/multidimensional healer and an Advanced Angelic Healing Practitioner. She writes inspirational, spiritual poems and poems on Social issues (mainly touching issues arising out of domestic-intimate partner violence). She takes her past childhood trauma experiences and weaves them into poetry. In her coaching and healing sessions, she uses EFT-tapping, writing prompts, photography, painting, and visualization techniques. She provides intuitive multidimensional healing, TwinFlame activation guided meditation, Angelic healing, Golden Light healing. Her hobbies include traveling, listening songs, photography, and reading. She had many spiritual experiences throughout her childhood, but her pregnancy and the dream related to her child evoked curiosity and took her to a much deeper level. She has a law degree from India and currently graduated from University of Massachusetts, Lowell with Master's in Criminal Justice. She currently works in a nonprofit organization and lives in Massachusetts, United States with her husband and 7-years young and handsome son.

ABOUT MY BUSINESS

Manoroma Mimi offers Holistic Coaching (using EFT-tapping, writing prompts, photography, painting, and visualization techniques), intuitive multidimensional healing, TwinFlame activation guided meditation, Angelic healing, and Golden Light healing.

Website
https://www.facebook.com/groups/317098352599753/
(Her Facebook Group: "ONE SOUL BEING - Wisdom from Mother Earth").

Facebook Personal Page
www.facebook.com/mimi.das.5059

Instagram
Mimi Das (@travelersoul_mimidas) • Instagram photos and videos

THANK YOU!

The many ways to connect with me more
• Activation and first guided healing session of Intuitive Multidimensional Healing.
• Discovery calls for Holistic Coaching (30 minutes).
• Accountability 1-on-1 and group zoom calls.
• *All bookings and consultations via Facebook messenger. *

Dawn
Pensack

YOU'RE TOO MUCH

I used to LOVE Tuesday mornings. My mastermind group and I got together every single Tuesday.

We'd share our wins. Support each other. Plan. And go forth making a difference in the world!

But on this particular Tuesday (September 7, 2021), it just wasn't the same. I could feel something was different.

I logged into Zoom as I always did but this time, I waited and waited.

I didn't think too much about it since I'm usually the last one to log in but I got this nudge that something was up.

We all exchanged our niceties ("Hey - how ya doing?" "How's the weather?") and still …

Something was off.

Then … Mary spoke up about 2 minutes into the call.

"Dawn, we have to talk".

"Ok - what's up?"

"We have some concerns with you."

Huh? Concerns? I was so confused. But I could feel the tension in the group and my body froze even though my instincts were telling me to RUN.

Run far.

Run fast.

Run NOW.

I thought to myself … "What on earth could this be about?"

Was there something I did wrong?

Was I not active enough in helping them?

Were they mad I was usually a few minutes late?

When I made the decision to stay on the call (and not jump off zoom!), I knew this could get really awkward really fast.

So, I did the first thing I could think of to protect myself and preserve the lessons I was meant to learn from this experience.

I floated above my body and wrapped myself in a protective pink bubble of love.

Pure. Unconditional. LOVE.

When I looked down at myself (wearing a red tank top with 'More Love' printed on the front), I smiled.

I reached down, gave myself a big high-five and whispered, 'Dawn, you got this! This is happening FOR you'.

And then I floated back up to observe what was about to unfold.

At this point, the women, Mary, Trudy, Sophie, and Kiera started going around the 'table'.

They started talking and this is what I heard.

"You're too energetic … "

"You're too passionate ..."

"You have SO many ideas! …"

"When you have an idea, you run with it faster than anyone I know..."

These phrases were usually followed by something unsupportive or something about how I'm making them uncomfortable …

"We just don't know how to help you anymore".

"You're exhausting me. How do you even SLEEP at night?!"

As I was listening to them, I became so confused.

They kept saying, "We're doing this with good intentions." "This is so uncomfortable for all of us".

As they talked, one after the other …

It hit me and a wave of pure gratitude washed through my body.

The healing and transformation work I had been SO committed to was helping me understand that what they were saying didn't resonate with me and I didn't have to accept any of this. I get to choose what I'm 'keeping' and 'deleting'. I actually started seeing their sentences as words floating across the screen and then I chopped off what I wanted to 'keep' and brought those words into my heart. The rest of the sentence was pushed away – disappearing into the air.

I felt empowered! It was like I was riding a horse (sitting in the most comfy saddle!) with a group of people who were complaining about how uncomfortable it is to ride a spiky porcupine. It just didn't make any sense to me.

And then the massive ah-ha moment came…

THEY WERE SHINING A LIGHT ON ALL OF MY BRIGHTEST GIFTS!

They were literally magnifying every single one of my gifts … many of which I wasn't fully allowing to come through and some of these gifts I hadn't even realized!

And even though my bright light was making them uncomfortable, I made a bold decision in this moment that

I was NOT going to let them suppress me, dim my light, or take away my passion & enthusiasm.

Knowing the power of words and how negative, unkind, and unsupportive this energy was, I grabbed an imaginary shield and started blocking anything they said that didn't fit into the context of who I KNOW I truly am.

At the very end, Trudy piped up (it looked like she just consulted an agenda) and said …

"So, Dawn, how are you going to fix this?"

The very FIRST thing that popped in my head was, " I'm not a broken, busted up vase. There's nothing to fix!" but in this state of shock & survival where my sympathetic nervous system was firing, I have NO idea what I actually said.

All my gifts started flashing before my eyes. My passion. My energy. My love. The way I encourage and support others. The courage I have to not stay stuck in something that's not serving my highest good. My creativity.

And seriously… did they actually want me to open up and be vulnerable by asking me this?! They just went around the group and did a rapid fire hot seat of, what they considered to be my limitations, weaknesses, and blindspots. They KILLED the psychological safety of the entire group - not just for me. But for all of them, too.

There was NO way I was actually going to share what I was thinking or feeling and I sure as heck wasn't going to allow them to tell me what my faults are and how I'm going to fix myself.

And Trudy again ... "So, what are you going to do moving forward?"

Again, the first thought that came through ... "Let you guys go. This group served its purpose but I'm ready to shine my light somewhere else."

Suddenly, I felt deeply sad for these women. This conversation wasn't helpful, encouraging, or supportive. Isn't that the foundation for a mastermind?

Not one of these women thought of approaching the situation differently – with compassion, understanding, or love.

I also know life is a mirror.

This experience helped me see times in my life when I judged others in an unfair, unkind way. And this realization hit me deep.

In my reflection, I also got a chance to dive even deeper into the magic of highly effective communication.

As my mom taught me ... speaking with kindness is always the best choice. Yes - it sure is!

Throughout this whole experience, I kept wondering why I co-created this experience in my life. Ironically, this happened at a time when I had so much clarity and excitement for what I was creating in my business, and so much MOMENTUM.

I felt like I was being kicked down when I was at my highest.

I kept asking myself questions. And I waited…

What lessons were coming through from this?

Was there a reason these lessons were delivered in this way?

What did I need to do moving forward?

Where is my soul being guided?

For a few hours after this experience, I let myself feel hurt, sad, and angry. I let myself feel ALL the emotions.

And then, September 8 came – the very next day.

I was participating in an event with over 120 people to learn more about how to facilitate powerful conversations, tap into the collective wisdom of a group, and create exponential change.

In one of the opening exercises, we were asked to choose a question from a list of questions that we'd like to reflect on and share with a small group.

The question that JUMPED out at me was, "What is your biggest gift that you can't wait to share with the world?"

Immediately, I thought about yesterday.

And my gifts - my passion, energy, enthusiasm, creativity, love.

In the small group, I shared a 30 second clip of what happened yesterday and how I felt minimized, unappreciated, and unseen BUT how this group put a spotlight on my greatest strengths, some of which I hadn't even realized! I also shared how I am NOT broken and don't need to be fixed - I need to lean into who I am and magnify my gifts even more!

The people in this group both shared how they felt this story deeply in their hearts. How it helped them remember a time when someone tried to dampen their spirits or knock them down and how it gave them an opportunity to heal an old wound.

I was shocked - yet again.

My story has this effect? Really?

We were soon kicked back to the main group to share with the whole group.

People were raising their hands, eager to share.

But I sat back. Waited.

And for some reason, I kept feeling a strong nudge behind me. Maybe an angel was whispering in my ear, "You need to raise your hand, too, Dawn".

I ignored it for a bit.

Then, I raised my hand.

I WAS PICKED!

Oh man, I started panicking. Sweating. Nervous.

This wound was still far from being healed and I knew the danger in sharing from a wound, not a scar.

What the heck was I gonna say?!

I decided to get present. Take a deep breath. And just share from my heart.

I DID IT.

I opened up.

I shared from my heart.

And the more I shared, the more clarity I got and the more I started remembering.

Right at the end when I shared about my realization that I'm not a broken plate that needs fixing, the tears came.

But the tears weren't only mine. Tears were flowing from so many others and hundreds of messages started coming through the chat.

It was overwhelming. In the most positive, loving way … overwhelming.

"Dawn - you can never make someone big by playing small."

"Dawn. you are not broken … accept yourself for who you are"

"Dawn you are perfectly made just the way you are. Your gifts and talents are unique and can be used in amazing ways to impact others the way other people cannot."

"Thank you Dawn for sharing ALL of who you are!"

"Congratulations Dawn for finding yourself and stepping into your purpose!"

"Fix the people you're spending time with! Nobody should be telling you to tone down your passion!"

People started sharing how much the story deeply impacted them.

They mentioned how it gave them the chance to see the parts of them that were ready to be healed and seen.

Graham mentioned how it gave him the opportunity to heal the part of him that was doing the judging - the part of him that may not have been so kind or compassionate in the past.

Lenny talked about how he remembered a time when he was tossed to the side by a group he respected when he most needed their support.

Dr. Harry told me how there are universal threads in this story and that I NEED to get it out there in a huge way. For kids. For adults. For EVERY human who was ever told they needed to be different from who they truly are.

Over the next few weeks, more opportunities, love, and light have come through my life than ever before.

I've had conversations with some of the most incredible people - people who believe in elevating one another, lifting each other up, and sharing so much positivity with this world.

THOSE are my people.

And those are YOUR people, too.

You deserve to be surrounded by people who see and APPRECIATE your gifts.

People who can help you see what you're not seeing and speak LOVE, light, and truth into your heart.

People who can guide you to realizing that you're so much stronger than you think.

People who can celebrate your wins with you and stand beside you when you're making more progress than you've ever had before.

Think back to a time when you felt unseen, unappreciated, or minimized.

Let yourself FEEL all the emotions that come up.

What part of you were you able to tap into so that you could access resilience and strength?

Thank everyone involved for giving you the opportunity to see how strong and courageous you really are.

And now, how will you spread your light, love, and passion with this world?!

Names have been changed

ACKNOWLEDGEMENTS

I'd love to acknowledge "the Mavens" for their incredible friendships and support in the early days of building my business. Brittney, Marie, Dawn, Jackie, Kim, Erica, you are all AMAZING and I'm so grateful for all the hours we spent brainstorming, sharing, celebrating, and growing. Thank you for believing in me - love you all so much!

ABOUT AUTHOR

Dawn Pensack is a former "burned out" middle school math teacher who left the classroom to heal and learn how to better manage stress after she struggled with chronic sickness. She became an EFT Practitioner and later became fascinated with the moon's cycle and how our energy and wellness is impacted as the moon goes through the different phases. She has helped hundreds of men and women connect to this unique energy as they learn more about themselves, align their work and relaxation to the lunar phase, and allow more ease and abundance into their lives.

ABOUT MY BUSINESS

I help visionaries and heart-centered humans align with the cycles of the moon to connect more deeply with themselves, each other, and universal energies so that they allow more abundance into their lives.

Website
www.dawnpensack.com

Facebook Personal Page
@dawnpensack

Instagram
@dawnpensack

THANK YOU!

I'd love to offer an opportunity for readers to learn more about how to welcome in more ease, flow, and abundance and grow their businesses faster by tuning in to their unique astrological signs. This is a free 30 minute session. You will Learn: 1. What your Sun Sign, Moon Sign, and Rising Star Sign are and what this means for you. 2. How to optimize and restore your energy based on your unique chart. 3. Discover how the Moon's energies will affect different areas of your life over the next THREE months 4. Identify what to RELEASE and what to FOCUS on to grow your business faster. The link to sign up is: https://www.dawnpensack.com/moonguidance

Serena
Chow

RESILIENCE

I grew up the eldest of four daughters in a three-bedroom one bath home in Portland, Oregon. That would be me, Teal, Lynn & Sherie. There are six years between Sherie and me. I think we grew up as a close family because we had such a small house. My mom, May, is my hero. I don't know how she managed a full-time teaching job, helped with billing for dad's pharmacy, AND managed a household! It was an experience to remember for life! She has always been there to encourage me to stretch beyond my comfort zone throughout my life. At nine years old, she signed me up to memorize & recite a poem to compete with other girls my age from different schools for a chance at being part of the Junior Rose Festival court for Portland's annual Rose Festival time. (I don't think I got past the first cut) She encouraged me to run for school secretary in 7th grade (my first taste of student government) and suggested I ask my friend Marsha Aust (who was very shy) to be my campaign manager. My campaign slogan was " Oka is OK, " and I became school secretary. I held many positions in student government in high school, all due to my mom's nudging me to run for school secretary in 7th grade. Throughout my school years leading up to college, she was always on the lookout for other opportunities for me to participate, which increased my self-esteem and well-roundedness.

Mom took us to church every week as well. Dad was working seven days a week at his pharmacy during those years, so he was either working, or when he closed on Sundays, that was his only day to relax. Those church growing years impacted my life and faith as a Christian, for which I'm forever grateful. Mom had grown up in church too, and church offered good values and a strong foundation. I think she knew that the spiritual foundation learned there would equip us for life. We did lots of local activities, including activities with Seattle churches.

We had a revolving door at our home in the high school/college years as our friendships expanded up through Seattle. We did a lot of church activities up there. When there were Asian tennis tournaments in either city, we always had folks staying over (we had a full basement, very cool in the summer, plus a pool table and pingpong table, which all the guys liked); it was very busy with all of us working, trying to enjoy our summers.

In fact, when we were little, and company would drop by right as she was making dinner, mom would tell us to take a few bites, say we were finished, and go downstairs and play, and that she'd feed us later! Imagine that.

My mom, Chinese, was not your quintessential Tiger Mom. Because she was an educator, she relied a lot on common sense (from my grandma, her mom, who singlehandedly raised her eight kids) and logical consequences. My mom was one of only two of her siblings to go to college. Other practical skills I learned from her were using coupons and watching the prices as the cashier rung items up to be sure they were right. I learned that last skill very quickly because of all the times I was sent back to the grocery store (2 blocks from home) to get a refund because they had overcharged us, embarrassing, to say the least. I learned to love cooking baking, how to clean and do laundry and keep our room clean. Those disciplines have stayed with me for life. Mom would always let me experiment with new recipes. Once it took me 6 hours to bake a loaf of French bread in our (single) oven, but she let me do it. Oh, and did I mention canning tomatoes and making dill and bread & butter pickles?! Yes, I'm a canner ☺ All of these skills helped me to love to have people over and developed my hospitality skills.

My mom also had a knack for striking up a conversation with anyone. And she really paid attention to engaging those that were shyer or overlooked. She knew exactly how they felt from her childhood years. That was from growing up and having very little but also being content with what they had.

Through those years growing up, I learned the art of hospitality and the art of connection. My mom just had the gift of gab...and being the oldest, I was around her the longest, and I guess that rubbed off on me too! My friends have commented over the years that they know they can call me when they're trying to find a resource, and I'll either know someone directly or can make a meaningful connection for them—I love that~gives me so much joy to help others, and I had the best example in observing mom and how she did that.

Because of her upbringing not having money, my

mom was never able to have music lessons, play sports in school, or do other extracurricular activities that we had. She had us all taking piano lessons starting at about age 9, and I have no idea how my dad got enough sleep because we started practicing at 6:30 a.m. before we left for school! She also gave us dance lessons (I tap danced for 6-8 years with one of my sisters) and then sports for some of my younger sisters in high school. Mom really knew how to make something out of nothing. She was a master of stretching a dollar, and one of the best things she ever had was a gift closet. She'd buy things on sale and stash them in there, and whenever we got invited to a birthday party, she'd always have something on hand. That concept stayed with me as I raised my kids. As a result, I have saved time and money.

So, let's talk about my dad, Shig. Quiet, Japanese American by descent, my dad was very hardworking. His dad worked in Eastern Oregon, building the railroad back in the day. Dad received his pharmacy degree from OSU, and soon after took & passed the CA Pharmacy board test to expand his job options. My aunt (mom's sister) & uncle lived in Anchorage, AK. My uncle was a doctor. He was planning to open a medical center and wanted my dad to run the pharmacy. Because there weren't a lot of jobs in Portland at the time, it was a great opportunity. So, he and my mom packed up their stuff, me and Teal, and drove up to Anchorage in our little VW. Lynn was born in Anchorage, and we soon returned to Portland because Teal had terrible asthma, and the climate in AK didn't help.

Back in Portland, dad worked for some other pharmacists but received a call one day from Art, a pharmacist that he had done an internship with while in pharmacy school. Art saw that there was an independent pharmacy (Nolan Rexall Drugs) for sale, and wanted to partner up with my dad to buy the business. Art's idea in the contract was to have a clause in there that my dad would buy him out within five years. What an amazing mentor and business partner he was for my dad.

I thought it was my mom that I inherited my entrepreneurial tendencies from, but after hearing my dad relay this story, I realized I inherited those qualities from him. Both he and my mom had strong work ethics that spilled over into my life, but from working at the drugstore, I saw what it took to run a business—good times as well as slow times. My dad had a lot of grit and determination to make it through those years. He kept his pharmacy open seven days a week and then went down to 6 days a week. I never heard him complain about business lagging, ever.

Once pharmacy chains started popping up in Portland, he continued to reduce his hours. Even though he couldn't compete with them on price, he competed in other ways, like serving the older Japanese (Isei) population by delivering their medications to their doorstep if they were housebound and couldn't get out. He would close the shop up at 9 p.m. and not get home until later because he made deliveries after hours. All the small independent pharmacies in Portland supported each other. If dad didn't have a particular drug, he could borrow from another pharmacy and replace it later.

Dad was a man of few words, but when he talked, we listened. And, he was so low key… he had to be with four, no five wild women that he lived with! He could have been in the Guinness Book of World records for the time it took him to get ready to go out with all of us. My folks added a ½ bath downstairs just so he could get into the bathroom upstairs!

My dad gave me my first real job. When I was 12 or 13 and had decent handwriting, I'd copy dad's (handwritten) customer information to 3X5 cards kept in these long file drawers that we took home from the store and spread out on the kitchen table. Each transaction was handwritten, one per line, front and back of a piece of lined notebook paper. He'd call and ask me to look it up in the files when he needed information. I started at $.50/side and worked my way up to $.75 over the next two years. By 9th grade, I worked the front register at the store after school. Our business was conveniently located on the bus line I took to high school. Without electronic technology, I had to calculate the change for every purchase. Then, I counted the change back into customers' hand so they would know that I had done the math correctly. My dad was a visionary, too—he set up accounts for all his regular customers and billed them monthly. That was a fun, monthly family activity--printing those thermal statements, stuffing them into envelopes, addressing, and putting stamps on them.

Growing up in the '60s was a complicated time. There was a lot of racism in our country at the time, and Portland was no exception. I remember one time Mom was yelling on the phone. My friend Melinda said something racist about me (I think it may have been her older brothers or maybe her mom, we girls were only 6 or 7 at the time) who lived around the corner up the alley from our house. After that (yelling) conversation she had on the phone, I was told I couldn't play with her anymore. Our town was predominantly white, and I remember a couple of boys following me home from school calling me Chink & Jap. I know it had to be my mom's strength of encouraging us to try new things and do our best, that those experiences had minimal effect on my self-worth.

Because of the strong belief that my mom had in me as a child growing up, none of those things really phased me in a negative way. In fact, I'm not sure how those comments didn't affect us. After all, my mom being Chinese & dad being a Nisei (2nd generation American Japanese) made for a difficult relationship, let alone marriage. Because my Auntie Lil had married my Uncle Mino (Japanese) already, when my parents got married, it was easier for my grandma to accept. My dad's family was sent to internment camp when he was 12. His three older siblings were yanked from high school, so I think it was more traumatic for them. Dad was more open as he got older to share about it, and grandkids' family history reports brought a lot of those experiences out. He was interviewed and recorded by the Oregon Historical Society to preserve that period in history. Senior President Bush made reparation for all the Japanese Americans who were interned with a $20,000 check back in the 1990s. My folks treated all of us girls and our families to a cruise to Alaska. That was a memorable trip.

My mom was always on the lookout for the marginalized in our community—whether it was giving a ride to a new single gal that went to our church because she didn't have a car, to "adopting" Lan, one of my mom's students, a single mom from Laos with a little boy. Mom was one of eight kids. Seven lived in Portland, so holiday gatherings were never less than 20-30 people. So, adding a few more people was never a problem. We always hosted Thanksgiving and Christmas Eve dinners. Mom invited Lan and her son to our Thanksgiving gathering one year soon after they had met. I remember Lan, with huge eyes, following my mom into our (tiny) kitchen where the spread of food was on the table. Mom introduced her to family members along the way, ensuring they got plates of food, and a place to sit. I'm pretty sure she sent food home with them as well. My mom continued her friendship with Lan. As a result, Lan completed both her Associate and Bachelor degrees, worked in the corporate world, and eventually sent her son to college. The friendship and hope that my mom shared with Lan through the years will continue to impact future generations of Lan's family that my mom will never see.

GOD DOESN'T WASTE ANYTHING WE LEARN

I know now that my mom's desire was for something better for us during those key formative years than what she had grown up with. She wanted me and my sisters to experience life to the fullest and have a strong foundation of Christian values. But, even if she didn't say she loved us all the time, her actions showed it, and she stood by us through thick and thin.

My entire family, including mom and dad, are all graduates of Oregon State University, Beaver nation! I was so fortunate to be recruited by IBM right out of business school there. I had to go an extra quarter because I had changed my major so many times, but during the course of those four years, it definitely paid off. Then, I landed a job in San Francisco, right in the heart of the Financial District. This was the first time in my life I really had wanted to find a job and live in Seattle. I had a lot of friends there, and it would have been a very comfortable move. So, I told God that I'd move anywhere for a job EXCEPT the Bay Area....He really has a sense of humor, and I was probably in shock as I prepared that month after graduating to plan my move south. I had one of my best friends from college, Gretchen, who was already working and living there, and she found a great three-bedroom flat for us to live in, along with a friend from high school. When my folks took me to the airport to board my United flight to San Francisco, it was a sad day. I'd not really ever seen my dad cry before, but he shed some tears did as we were saying goodbye. I think I cried the entire flight. I was the first to fly the coop, but I'm not sure it got any easier. While my folks were sad about me leaving to start my new life, I'm sure it was a financial relief not to have three of us in college all at once. My folks paid cash for all of us to go to college, which gave us such a strong start to our new lives. I never realized what a gift it was until I had my own kids and started planning their college funds.

One of the other qualities my mom instilled in me was that it's not necessarily about the grades but about the experience—translate that into playing board games. As a result, I never had a hard time losing, and it's because of this guiding principle I learned growing up.

I loved my corporate job. I had no idea what I would do with a bachelor's degree in business and a minor in computer science. But God knew. He placed me in the Systems Supplies Division (SSD), where I was trained to sell computer supplies for all of the equipment that IBM manufactured. Of course, we were always the most expensive, so I applied all of the things I had learned growing up those two years that I was in that job. I had to learn how to cold call, conduct a sales call, and use my strengths in the sales process to win contracts over a competitor whose prices were lower. I had a blast! I had ok grades in college, but when I landed in the corporate world, it was cause and effect right in front of me. My own hard work translated to the bottom line of my paycheck. I thrived. My role in the SSD wasn't my ideal job, so I began looking for another career path within IBM. During college, I had done a lot of secretarial work for companies that would call my mom at her junior college asking if she had students to work summer intern programs. No HR departments back in the day. The head secretary to the branch managers did all the HR. And I knew how valuable secretaries were, and took good care of all of our admin — they worked really hard. So I landed a Systems Engineer (SE) job and spent seven years working in various capacities in that branch office. The coolest thing about my IBM career was that I was able to use all that administrative experience from my college summer jobs in all my sales jobs. As well as the industry knowledge, I soaked up working for so many different companies. God doesn't waste anything we learn. I had a very successful sales career at IBM.

We started our family in 1990 and had our daughter Stephanie, and then our son David in 1992. I started looking for something to do from home to bring in some income, and I tried a couple of things that didn't work out. When exploring homeschooling options for the kids, I stumbled upon an educational book company, Usborne Books. I fell in love with the books, and the kids loved the books I brought home from a conference. Growing up, we all were bookworms. We'd each have our own bag of library books for our 2-3 week car vacation, and at the end of the time, my sisters and I would have read all the books each of us had brought along. In fact, our libraries in Portland were so much better than our local library where we were living in the East Bay. I got a reality check about what our local school systems were like in California when I visited the main branch of our county library after the kids were born. It was about the size of a typical branch library that I grew up with. One thing led to another, and we ended up homeschooling both our kids. I homeschooled Stephanie through high school, she ended up at UCLA for four years. David attended a private Christian high school and achieved his dream of becoming an Effects Artist (special effects for movies).

I WENT TO WORK ON MYSELF

It was 2010, nearing the end of the first recession, both kids were in college, and I had spent 16 years homeschooling and selling Usborne Books. In that time, I sort of lost that belief and confidence that I'd grown up with and also the success I'd had working in corporate. I worked a lot of hours for not that much income and time away from the family. So in my mind, I was thinking about looking for something else I could do from home that didn't require all the overhead my Usborne business had and that I could actually help team members who really needed extra money. That's when I got the phone call. I thought it was a mom asking if I'd be on campus the next day for the preschool book fair I was running. Instead, she asked if I was open to looking at another business. It was my business partner Trish of 12 years.

I was so excited; their business model made complete sense—simply switch where I was shopping and spend those same dollars at a different store. Of course, online shopping back in 2010 wasn't as popular as it is today, but I quickly found out how convenient it was. Saved me a ton of time. And, I loved the product quality. What's funny is that when I started with Melaleuca, I knew it was going to require a lot of personal development. But, I had no idea how deeply that would impact me. I quickly advanced my business in my first 18 months, and then I hit a flat spot that lasted nine years. Those years were what strengthened me the most, and I still received a paycheck each and every month for my customer's shopping.

Have you ever felt like you didn't deserve success? That is how I felt a lot of the time. Where had all that belief gone that I had during my years in corporate? Maybe it had gone by the wayside in those early years of raising the kids, as now I was identified more by who my kids were than what I was doing/accomplishing on the job. We also were struggling with being empty nesters and having not been diligent about weekly dates (expensive for a babysitter, and then paying for dinner, etc.); we hadn't nurtured and fostered our marriage relationship over the years. There was turmoil on the homefront. I wondered if counseling might help. In 2014 when I told my mom I was considering counseling for me, she said it's about time! I nearly fell over. Anyways, that was the best thing I could have done for myself. I went to work on myself. I couldn't change my husband. Those next 18-24 months changed my life. On the first day we met, my therapist said that her objective was to work herself out of a job with me…and I said Great! We hit it off immediately. I saw her every week for at least a year and then went twice a month. At this point, our discussions were starting to become more of a business mindset coaching session (I had the tools to deal with the interpersonal stuff at home, had developed healthy boundaries once again, and confidence to hold to them). When I went down to seeing her once a month, it became difficult for her to fit me in. One day, I realized I hadn't seen her in two months and was feeling okay with things. I knew it was time to lay her off. On the day I announced I was laying her off permanently, we both had a good laugh, and I felt great inside.

So, I kept plugging away, year after year, working my Melaleuca business and opening shop club accounts for many families. Then 2020 happened. Frank, our CEO, knew COVID was coming to the US. We have a manufacturing facility in Shanghai, and corporate had been dealing with it at the end of 2019. I think I had COVID in February 2020. So, I committed to a Fast Track team for 90 days, starting February 1. Fast Track is an annual (voluntary) team competition; EVERYONE on the team of four must hit their personal goals in order for the team to earn the reward. (It was a three-day trip to a top all-inclusive resort in Playa del Carmen, Mexico). I gave our team permission to nudge (kick) me if they needed to because I didn't want to be the weak link that prevented us from all earning the trip. Trish and I strategized that this could be what might push my business to the next level of Senior Director.

With our company's business model, you can affect business change in 90-day windows. The tipping point for me was when coach Ben said to me that he believed in me in March. I've had a lot of great coaches in my years with the company who were always very supportive of me, but hearing Ben say those four words, "I believe in you," that inspired me to go for it. Working toward getting into momentum is like that that huge stone grist mill, you know, the one that has a donkey or mule pushing the long log that takes forever to start the large round stone rolling on top of the flat stone. Once you have it going, it's much easier to accelerate—you're in motion, in momentum. So after that conversation with Ben, I kicked into high gear, and here are the results. No change after 30 days, but after 60 days, I double advanced my business for the first time in 9 years, and then two months later, I advanced to Senior Director. I kept pinching myself to be sure it was real! My business was in momentum. It was an incredible feeling to have helped so many folks gain access to products during the height of the pandemic and also to help businesses and families generate additional income if their jobs had been eliminated or hours drastically reduced as a result of the pandemic.

The amazing thing about Melaleuca's business model was that I still received a check for customers shopping during those nine years of not believing I deserved success.

COVID hit the US, and then the shutdown happened. Melaleuca had all the things families were looking for – natural products, American-made, no supply chain issues for hand sanitizer or disinfectant, and doorstep delivery when people didn't want to go out shopping. They helped hundreds of families get safer, natural products into their homes during that unprecedented time, and the majority haven't gone back to shopping in person.

I've never been so grateful for a company that takes care of all the Little Guys. Our country and its economy were built by thousands of Little Guys.

ACKNOWLEDGEMENTS

Heartfelt thanks to my mom and dad for raising me to be the individual I am today, and to my sisters, Teal, Lynn, and Sherie, without whom I would never have experienced the fun, daring, or mischievous adventures of growing up together. Bravo to dad who put up with all of us too! Thank you to my wonderful husband Jon, who has put up with all my escapades, mistakes, and triumphs over the years!

ABOUT AUTHOR

Serena grew up in Portland, Oregon. After college she moved to the San Francisco Bay area where she still resides. She has been married to her husband Jon for 34 years. They have two grown children--Stephanie (Yeah) and David; and three grandchildren, Rachel, Nathaniel, and Daniel Yeah. Her hobbies include cooking, baking, reading, bird watching, traveling, and singing with the Blackhawk Chorus; a 30 year-old community chorus.

ABOUT MY BUSINESS

Melaleuca, The Wellness Company is a 36 year old, U.S. based, natural, essentials manufacturer. They specialize in helping individuals & business owners put a solid Plan B in place during these uncertain times. In addition, they educate individuals & families how to maintain a healthy immune system and overall better physical wellness.

Website
www.melaleuca.com

Facebook Personal Page
https://www.facebook.com/serena.chow.773

THANK YOU!

If you need a Plan B for your family, or desire improved health (lose weight, obtain healthier products for your home, etc.), I'm offering a complimentary overview of Melaleuca to see how we can help you. Please email me your contact information, a good time to call, and we'll connect~

Lori
Keefer

MY SUPERPOWER IS ME!

My Mom passed my baby brother to me. We could all smell his dirty diaper. We could all hear his cry's echoing loudly throughout the stairwell of our apartment building. She had just come back up the three flights of steps toting a crowbar she had retrieved from the trunk of the little Fiat car. "Stand back," she said matter of factly to my sisters and me. If I had to choose a descriptor of my Mom at that moment, it would have been resolved and determined. Our eyes went wide as she swung back and CRACK! The echo of her hitting the apartment door with that crowbar was loud, yet it made no sound as we watched her determination to get her children into the apartment. Finally, the hole was large enough for her hand to reach in to unlock the door. In we all went, my brother was changed and fed, and we went on about our day. It's over 40 years later, and I can still remember the feeling of amazement and smell that dirty diaper. I learned that my Mom would literally break down doors for her family. It's a lesson I model each and every day for my own.

I was born in a small, rural town in Ohio, where my family was an integral part of all the townsfolk 'comings and goings. My earliest memories are watching my Dad butcher the pigs we raised, helping my Mom can vegetables, and standing on the dirt pile out front performing to my imaginary audience. "Life is not fair. It never was and never will be." Papa (my grandfather) said to me many times. "Life is not fair, but you have to live it the best you can, and then you will die, and someone else will wear your shoes," he said after he'd draw on his pipe or cigar. I can still smell that cigar smoke and hear his gravelly voice. I believe then he was trying to teach his granddaughter that complaining would not accomplish much except annoy other people. That saying has stuck with me to this day. I have repeated it thousands of times to myself and others.

"Don't whine about it; find a solution!" My Dad often said this phrase when one of us kids came to him with a problem. Whether it was a homework problem, a prized toy that was broken, or trying to make our budget stretch farther, every problem had a solution. I learned as a kid that there was a solution to just about any dilemma or situation that might present itself. Does your younger brother keep stealing your barbie dolls? No problem, we just found a cabinet with a lock where we kept them. No money to buy Halloween costumes? No worries, we can just make our own! It was the spoken lessons from my Dad and grandfather, combined with my Mom's unspoken examples of resolve and determination, that determined a big part of who I am today.

My Dad joined the Air Force when I was six years old. "Davey! You need to do something with your life" is what my Papa told my Dad just prior to that. Dad would say to me when I was an adult that he wasn't quite sure what his father meant by that, but he joined the Air Force and knew he could better support his family. My childhood years took me from that rural farm to many places worldwide as the Air Force stationed Dad at one base and then the next. We never had much money-wise, especially in the early years. Mom would mend clothes to pass down from one kid to the next. Going to thrift stores was always an adventure for us! But, we never really thought to complain. We were together, and we were happy.

One constant in my life throughout my Dad's military career and beyond was family. It didn't matter where in the world we were, what challenges we faced, how little or much money we had, or how old we were. My family has always come first and always. If I had to identify my primary value of who I am to a core, it is family. I am my family. My family is me. We are intertwined.

Growing up, I watched Mom take care of our family while Dad worked. She'd divvy up the paycheck between envelopes to ensure we had food for our bellies and bills got paid. I still use a modified envelope system for our money management today. The four of us kids were often together even though there was a nine-year difference from the oldest to youngest. This remained even into my high school years.

We moved to Maryland when I was in the eighth grade. I had attended schools in six states and two countries by then. I remember coming home from Band Camp the summer before my Sophomore year and Dad telling me he and Mom were separating and getting divorced. Mom moved out to a small but nice apartment. I remember helping her finish a dresser she had bought at Home Depot. She couldn't afford to buy a new one, so she purchased an unfinished one and did it herself. That dresser currently stores my clothes today. I remember Dad being gone a lot. He reclassified from enlisted to an officer, and we moved into Officer's Housing. That was when I became a surrogate mom to my three siblings.

Dad was gone a lot between work and school and dating. My brother was only a little older than I was when Dad first enlisted. I quickly learned how to manage high school, marching band, a babysitting job, and three kids (two of them still in elementary school). I had learned those lessons of never complaining, resolve and determination well. I was cook, housekeeper, homework helper, fight breaker, clothes mender, shoulder for crying on, and Chief boo-boo kisser. I could cut my Dad's hair with military precision and iron his uniform creases with a sharpness that could cut butter. I am sure I complained some, but it was what we did. We were family. Family always supported family. I had my friends, and marching band was my life. So I didn't miss out on anything.

ON MY OWN

A year after I graduated high school, my Dad was living in Sicily in his new job as head of the communications squadron at the Air Base there, and my Mom was moving to Germany with her Army husband. I was 19 and alone for the first time in my life. The closest family was hundreds of miles away. The lessons I learned growing up served me well. I had a full-time job, went to college part-time, my apartment, and paid all my bills on time.

I was dating someone who I thought, at the time, was the love of my life. I am sure I appeared quite happy to anyone looking. I thought I was happy. I now know that those seven years were with someone who was very controlling and verbally abusive. He slowly crushed my self-esteem. He slowly molded my thoughts to coincide with his. I am very thankful he tired of me and broke it off. My best friend was my savior. She was an abuse survivor herself, and she would not stop until I started going out again.

I lost weight, bought new clothes, and joined a BBS (bulletin board systems were digital bulletin boards where we could dial in from our computer and modem and exchange messages). This particular one was for adults only; we even had to provide the organizer with a photo of our driver's license to prove we were over 21 years old. We chatted online and met in public spaces for safety. I started getting out and making new friends.

It was through this BBS that I met my husband, Jerry. I'd spend hours at my computer, telephone cradled in my modem, chatting with him online. I can still hear the tones of the modem as it dialed in and connected. I can hear the hum of my old dot matrix printer as it printed out the conversation log so I could re-read them over and over. We eventually moved on to talking on the phone. He had separated from his current wife a few months prior, and his daughter was the apple of his eye. He always shared things about her. I remember our first official date quite well. The movie Snow White had just been re-released on VHS tape. He had just bought it for his daughter, and we were talking about how we both loved Disney movies. It was November 1, 1994. He couldn't come the night before because he was out trick-or-treating with his daughter. He brought the video, I put it on, popped popcorn, and we spent the entire night facing each other on the sofa and just talking and talking and talking. I think we both knew we had found our soulmate that night.

Ours was a typical love story. All worked around his six-year-old daughter. She was the same age I was when Dad joined the Air Force. She was about the same age my brother was when I started taking care of him while Dad worked. Jerry was going through a tough divorce (which is putting it mildly). Even today, I get angry at the stress his ex-wife put on their daughter. There were physical bruises on occasion and visible signs of mental abuse. I can forget about lies, deception, name-calling, and threats toward myself, Jerry, and his family. I cannot, nor will I ever, forgive someone for willingly harming a child. However, I am incredibly proud of how his daughter has matured and become the most amazing woman and mother despite all of that.

It was clear from the start that my new boyfriend had a family that believed in family. They lived in a home that once belonged to his grandparents. There were family game nights. There was lots of laughter around the kitchen table. Jerry's mother's laugh will forever be ingrained in my memory after she had just one-up someone playing a game. I would listen to him chat with his sister on the phone. She was his confidant, big sister, ally, and sounding board. I watched him crumble when we came home from the beach to find out she was missing, only later discovering her husband had murdered her. We were not married, but he was my family. Family is family.

A FAMILY OF MY OWN

Jerry and I married on July 4, 1997. We always said that if we could get through his awful divorce and the murder of his sister, we could do anything together! So we made our home in his little 900 square foot duplex. My paycheck supported his daughter and us since most of his paycheck went to the divorce lawyer. We were happy. We had fun being a family. We enjoyed doing things together. We dreamed of our future.

We later became the third generation to own his childhood home, and that was where we added to our family, and our girls were born. I will NEVER forget the feeling that washed over me when the doctor first placed my daughter in my arms. I knew why my Mom did what she did in that split second. I instantly knew that I would guide, protect, teach and love these tiny humans with my entire being. I stopped working and became a stay-at-home mom. We went without things to stretch our budget. Jerry and I have always hungered for the new technology. We bought our first digital camera when our daughter was born. In the first year of her life, we took over 10,000 photos. Yes, you read that right! I grew up watching Dad take pictures of "our memories." My family grew up hearing Dad say over and over, "Let's Make Some Memories." A memory in your head is terrific. A memory recorded in a photo or video is even better!

We moved to Pennsylvania right before our oldest started Kindergarten. Although I believe all the moving around as a child helped me become who I am today, I wanted my children to stay put through their grade school years. They both started and graduated from the same school district. I was the typical stay-at-home Mom. I served on the PTA from elementary through graduation. I volunteered at the school, taking all the candid photos for the yearbook and even creating the yearbook for several years when the girls were in elementary school. As my Mom was for me, I was my girl's Girl Scout Leader. Many called me "Mama Keefer" as I chaperoned the football games and band competitions. I was the proud band mom. I learned how to advocate hard for both of them to ensure the school was serving them best. I continued traditions from my childhood. We had our family game nights. We had our adventures both at home and on vacation. They played in the mud and had fun dressing all up for the dances at school.

I admit. During my girls 'school years, there were some times that the Mama Lion had to come out. It is super frustrating when you know your child is struggling in school only to have a teacher tell you that stricter discipline is the answer. It is equally disappointing when you have a child with a medical crisis, only to be let down by the school until you force them to accommodate as required by law. I could write an entire book on these things. But they are both of my daughter's stories to tell, and I will respect their privacy. Just know, I was and am incredibly proud at the perseverance of both of my daughters that they not only graduated high school with honors, but they both received top scholarships at their top choice of colleges.

When Jerry turned 50, we started to focus on the next chapter of our life together. The girls were in middle and high school, so we knew we were quickly closing in on empty nesters. His job was a good one and would provide many great retirement benefits. However, we knew we wanted more so that we could do more. We discovered that we loved having adventures and traveling together as we got older. We loved traveling with our girls. We also found areas in our community that we loved to help with both our time and money.

Jerry and I took our love of storytelling, combined it with his lifelong love of cars, and started a photography business. I knew starting a business would not be easy. I had watched my Dad do it a couple of times. Nevertheless, I pulled from my upbringing of resolve, determination, finding the solution, and knowing that life was not fair and dug in my heels.

My husband is a 56-year-old Hot Wheels fanatic! We even own a real-life Limited Edition Hot Wheels Camaro. We knew, in the beginning, we wanted to be high-end automotive photographers. To say we encountered lots of naysayers is putting it mildly. Well-known and successful photographers kept telling us there was no money in photographing cars. I admit the first few years, we hemorrhaged money. Our confidence took many hits.

We signed up for a photography conference at the recommendation of a friend. It was in that group that we met Paul & Melissa. I saw a post in the Facebook group about a course he was offering that taught how to provide a Santa Experience. Christmas has always been one of my most favorite times of the year! I simply love the excitement, wonder, and joy of the season. So we bought their Santa course and began what has proven to be the best decisions we have made for us both personally and for our professional careers.

We met them for drinks and dinner at the hotel bar at that photography conference. Their genuine willingness to help us succeed was mesmerizing. That evening over Lemon Drops and chicken tenders, we mapped out a rough marketing strategy that we still use over six years later. Yes, there was drawing and writing on napkins involved. As a result, we have established Jerry as a personal brand and expert in the automotive art industry. He is known worldwide and has art on loan to three museums. In addition, we use our skills to give back to non-profit organizations like the Chip Miller Amyloidosis Foundation and Veteran's causes.

I honed my photography skills and became a branding photographer, helping business owners create images to market themselves and their businesses. I enjoyed learning about their business, why they did what they did, and their personal lives that would be part of their brand. I also discovered my love of teaching around this time. I enjoy speaking to groups and helping them learn how to use their own stories to develop their brand to attract their perfect client and repel those that won't ever buy from them. I discovered that many small business owners and entrepreneurs had no clue how to market themselves beyond the "buy my thing" advertising. I worked this into my photography packages so my branding clients would know how to use the photographs I delivered to them. Even with all that work, I still would watch client after client pay me for photos only never to see them used.

WE ARE RESILIENT

In 2017, things quite literally started crashing down around me, and I felt like my world was ripping apart at the seams. My oldest daughter had a major medical crisis; my youngest daughter felt left out and forgot, and my Dad received his fourth cancer diagnosis with fewer than three years to live. I spent many nights crying myself to sleep with worry and sadness. I was getting ready to turn fifty. I didn't know if one of my daughters would finish high school, and I was heartbroken that I missed spending time with my other daughter. Doctors gave my Dad a 10% chance of making it three more years. I was so sad. I felt like all my hopes and dreams were crumbling down around me, and I had hit a brick wall.

If our family is anything, it is resilient. My daughter DID graduate high school and went off to college with many smiles. I spent time with my youngest and watched her come into her own. She auditioned and made the team for a competition color guard. Their show "Stand By Me" would be symbolic in many ways. They were on track to win first place in national champs when the global pandemic happened, and their season was cut abruptly short. My daughter, feeling left out, would have a very different high school experience than everyone before her. My Dad had terminal cancer. Knowing that what could be my Dad's last year or two with us would be spent apart wholly crushed me. Family is everything. Three Christmases in a row, we could not be with Dad. Even now, I am heartbroken at the loss of that physical time with him.

Once again, I found our solution. We started up our "family quarantine chats" over zoom each Friday. I recorded each one. Each week, we gathered around our computer screens and shared stories, laughed, commiserated, and kept each other sane. I haven't watched any of the recordings now that Dad is gone, but they will one day be an excellent way to remember him.

The pandemic shut our business entirely down. We lost thousands of dollars of business when we canceled several large contracts. We were very thankful that Jerry still had his full-time job. Even during a pandemic, the power grid still needed operators to run it. My upbringing taught me that you couldn't spend time focusing on the negative. You couldn't whine. We must find a solution.

While many around us were complaining and whining about losing money, we started thinking about ways to work regardless of our aging bones, physical location, and the new need for social distancing. Our automotive fine art will always remain. Cars do not carry viruses, and it's easy enough to distance us from their owners when the need arises. Plus, the process of creating the art is as much a part of my husband as is his eye color. He used the shutdown to hone his craft further, create some proprietary photography accessories, and develop an entirely new process of creating his art. We used the shutdown to perfect how he makes the fine art and rebrand into what we envisioned for the next phase of the business. We decided to niche down completely. We are only going to create fine art.

I would stop marketing for the high school senior, headshots, branding, and other "people" sessions. I admit I was sad at first. It is hard to let go of something that you have loved doing. But with all the hours spent home alone while we socially distanced, we did a lot of talking, researching, and going over our financials. We had decided this was the best way forward for the photography side of our business. But what did that mean for me? We were getting rid of the parts of our business that were primarily me.

FINDING MYSELF

I count the pandemic as a true blessing to help me find myself. During those long months of social distancing, I had many hours to think about what I wanted to do with the next chapter of my life. I had many options. I could simply be Jerry's wife, run the house, support the kids in college and hang with my friends. That was a great option. I had always been a "support" person most of my life. But was that enough for me? Did I need more?

We decided to invest over $15,000 and hire a personal business coach. We thought at the time that we needed a fresh perspective and left our original business coaches. We wanted to be able to stretch our fine art business, and I wanted to expand my teaching and coaching. When news of the pandemic across the globe started trickling into our news cycles, this coach invited me to join a group of fellow photographers delving into the essential oil world. Initially, I enjoyed the group. The group frequently met on zoom to plan our strategy. I knew I was not a salesperson like most of the others in the group. It is not just in my personality. We agreed I would do the training for the group and our downlines in return for them placing people under me as my income stream. I was patient. I knew how the system worked for this company and understood that there was a process for stacking people for the most income potential. Like most things I do, I jumped in and started working. I created content and training that everyone loved. After a while, I started noticing things that bothered me. Comments were made that started to weigh heavy on me and went against my values. After many months of countless hours and thousands of dollars on my part, someone from leadership crossed a line I was not willing to forgive or accept.

I have deep-rooted values in ethical business practices that I will not cross. I also have specific values about friendship and leadership that won't be wavered. These are values instilled in me growing up in a military family and modeled to me by both my parents. Going into the details of exactly what happened would serve no purpose other than bad-mouthing that person. She knows what she did because I told her when I informed her that I was leaving the group. I only mention it now because I believe that this happening was a big part of the process of me finding myself.

The month all that happened was a tough one for me. Discovering someone you trusted and admired could behave in a way so entirely against your core values is disheartening. The grief process I experienced is much like a death. I needed to move on quickly before it consumed me and brought me down. What should I do next? Who was I going to be? I craved something that was mine. I wanted to make my mark on the world. I loved working with Jerry on the fine art business, but he was the master behind the art. I had been the support person all my life and felt I needed something that I was the lead. So I started making my list of my various zones of genius.

I went back to my business roots and decided to join a high-level mastermind led by Paul and Melissa. They were two people I greatly admire, both as friends and business owners. They had helped guide us in our photography business, and I had watched them grow several successful multi-six-figure businesses themselves. But, most importantly, their core values aligned with my own.

I knew I wanted to teach. With Jerry's retirement around the corner, I wanted to teach regardless of where we were physically located in the world. I worked with our business mentors and those in my high-level mastermind to clarify what exactly my part in this business would become. I contemplated a variety of topics. Then, one day on one of our virtual mastermind retreats, Paul said something that resonated like a ton of bricks in my mind. He told the group that morning to "Make a decision. Take action." I wrote it down in big letters in my bullet journal. I have looked at that page many times since. He and his wife, Melissa, explained that whatever we decide to do today for our business does not have to be that way in 5 years. That took the pressure off of me to develop an online business that would be the perfect fit for my family and me. I now understood that it could morph, change, and adapt as I or my clients needed. So that day I made my decision. I started taking action.

I had so many life experiences to draw from, but I kept asking myself, "What is my superpower?" I even wrote on a sticky note that I stuck on my monitor, "What is my zone of genius?" Then, after many months of testing things out, I had my own "smack myself upside the head" moment.

MY SUPERPOWER IS ME!

My superpower is ME. I know that now. I guess I always knew this but never said it out loud or owned it until I started working through the process of what the next chapter of my life would tell. I have spent my life seeing all of the parts of something and then seeing how they fit together. Have you ever watched one of those movies or TV shows where actors visualize the numbers or pieces floating in front of their eyes as they work out the answer? That is me when it comes to a content plan, launch plan, how to pay the bills, or rearrange my house. Yes, I can literally see my sofa moving across the room in my mind. The same goes with all the pieces of my content and how they fit into my marketing funnel.

I looked at what I had been doing in our photography/fine art business. I pulled out and printed the emails back and forth with those past branding clients and looked at their common questions and concerns. How did we get the clients we did? What made them buy from us? I documented the system that we use and noted where I had made changes and improvements over the years. Next, I started asking other business owners where they struggled regarding content creation and social media. I wanted to know if and where they struggled with using content to get the clients they wanted. Several common themes fit perfectly with what I wanted to teach.

At the urging of my mentors, I leaned in heavy. I decided to take my stand. I remember one coaching call when Paul told me that I already knew all that I needed to know. Melissa kept telling me to take what I did for our photography business and translate that into my online coaching. They had mentored us into becoming profitable and thriving in a photography niche many others told us would never make us money (boy were all those naysayers wrong!!). I trusted their faith and knowledge. I started making my plans. I set my goals. I took action.

Conversation and relationships are Queen. Content is something to talk about with your audience. When I looked at how we attracted the clients in our fine art business, it all boiled down to the relationships and conversations with people. The intentional and purposeful conversations we started reigned supreme. I can trace each client back to a couple of very deliberate steps we took, conversations we had, relationships we cultivated.

I have so many life experiences to draw from, but those two topics kept coming back around in my head. Conversations and Relationships. I knew I had found my thing. The more I worked on this, the more excited I became. I started teaching business owners about using social media to help grow their businesses. Each time, the light bulbs I saw turn on over their heads gave me energy. My soul is fed simply from their amazement at the simple things I teach that can help boost their reach and engagement.

I will admit I am not the most prominent expert on social media. I started following the experts and soaking up their knowledge like a sponge. I also decided that I did not want to be known as the social media girl. I wanted to help people create content. I wanted to help people create content that sounded like them and not like templates. I wanted to help people create content that got them more clients. I wanted to help women business owners learn how to purposefully and intentionally have those conversations and build relationships with people that would consistently grow their business.

I looked at what we had done in our photography business and started translating it into what would help advance my coaching business. Yes, those words and images began flying around in front of my eyes again. Friends faces, intentional words, goals, numbers, and colors started arranging before my eyes as I formulated my plan.

I knew I needed to place myself around supportive and action-forward-thinking business owners. I wanted to surround myself with women like myself. I remain in the circles necessary for our photography business. Still, I knew if I wanted to impact the world with my superpower, I needed to surround myself with other women like me. So I re-joined Polka Dot Powerhouse and started doing what I love, having those conversations and building relationships. While I needed to network to grow my business, I also needed the fellowship with other women like me. My children were now adults. It was time to step aside as their counselor, tear wiper, scraped knee fixer, and chief worrier and step into my next chapter.

I founded my online membership using all of the principles and values that make up my superpower (me). First, I teach business owners how to create content that sounds like them, not someone else's template. Second, I help business owners learn how to use this content purposefully and intentionally to get the clients they want and repel the ones they don't. Finally, I help business owners gain confidence in having those conversations (in person and virtually) that build the relationships necessary to grow their business. Each week as I work with my clients, I see the small wins they are each making as they make the critical mindset shifts around their content and business. Most importantly, I get to see them start to really enjoy their business as they stop being overwhelmed with what to say and shape their content to serve their needs.

Over the last decade of my life, I have learned that you can succeed when staying true to your core values. Life will always throw you lemons. Life is not fair. Never was and never will be. As my daughters were learning to become adults and stretch their wings to fly on to their journey of life, I was discovering myself. Family. Tradition. Storytelling. Along with my lifelong quest for Adventure, Freedom, and Knowledge. They are who I am at my core.

The lessons I've learned, especially from dealing with real-life situations and building relationships, have allowed us to build a profitable photography and fine art business. It took focus, keeping our eye on the goal, sticking to our core values, and being faithful to what we wanted to do: high-end automotive photography and teaching. We love to preserve the history of all things automotive by intertwining the car and collector's story in an heirloom to pass down to future generations. People around the world recognize Jerry for his fine art. We enjoy traveling around the country for commissioned jobs. He has art published in several international magazines. We are very proud to have some of Jerry's art displayed at several museums (one a Smithsonian Affiliate).

As I continued on my quest to find myself, I continued to learn from my mentors and friends, Paul & Melissa, the power of mentorships, encouragement, and guidance. In addition, I have surrounded myself with my fellow Polka Dot Sisters, who also encourage and guide me on my journey. With my coaching business growing, my husband has recognized all the behind-the-scenes stuff I did in our photography business. While I will always rejoice in the wins of my members when they start applying what I teach, it is really special when your husband recognizes the good you're doing and not only comments on it but shares within his circles. I am thankful and grateful for his support. These all combined have helped me fully step into the mentoring role and pay it forward with the business owners in my membership and courses.

My legacy started as a small-town farm girl, continued as a girl traveling the world with my military Dad and family, my marriage to Jerry and birth of our family, and pursuing our dreams of building our businesses based on inspiration, encouragement, and gratitude.

"When you have a problem, don't whine about it. Find a solution." By watching my Mom and Dad, I learned that you can take those lemons and make lemonade with resolve, determination, perseverance, focus, and gratitude. I have created The Content Creator Club™ for those women like me who want to learn how to use the powerful story of who they are to invite and engage with people to grow their business in person and online. I'd love for you to join me!

ACKNOWLEDGEMENTS

I have to start by thanking my parents, David and Mary. As I reach middle age, I now understand that they modeled many of my life lessons when I was a child. You taught me how to put what matters first, how to talk to people, how to be my own person and so much more. You started molding who I would become as an adult. As my parents started the mold, my children, Teresa and Victoria, helped shape the mold. Learning how to parent and watch them grow into their wonderful young adults has indeed shaped who I am now. Paul and Melissa have helped shape my professional mold in bold, distinct ways. Their unwavering guidance and support have not only boosted my confidence but help shape my business values into what they are today. Of course, no acknowledgment would be complete without mentioning the support of my husband, Jerry. He has stood by my side through the rough times, the sad times, the wonderfully special times, and the boring times. We have laughed, argued, cried, and rejoiced as we navigated through the last quarter-century. I am genuinely looking forward to the next quarter-century and all that it may hold.

ABOUT AUTHOR

Lori Keefer is the creator of The Content Creator Club™. Lori uses her core values of Family and Storytelling combined with her quest for Freedom, Knowledge, and Adventure to guide her purpose. She strives to help female entrepreneurs overcome being overwhelmed when creating content grow their business(es) while still having time to do what makes them happy. She also co-owns a photography fine art business with her husband, where they use proprietary techniques and equipment to create high-end automotive art that has gained them recognition around the globe. When Lori is not educating or photographing, she enjoys spending time with her family. She's a proud mom, devoted poodle-owner, lover of tea, and her current passion project is preparing for the next chapter in her and her husband's life, retirement. She enjoys serving on the leadership team of her local chapter of Polka Dot Powerhouse and helping raise money for veterans' causes with her husband.

ABOUT MY BUSINESS

Lori coaches female entrepreneurs on how to create content that sounds like them, not someone else's template. She enjoys helping them stop being overwhelmed and become more confident in their messaging to reach the clients they want and repel the ones they don't.

Website
www.LoriKeefer.com

Facebook Personal Page
https://www.facebook.com/lorikeefer2

Instagram
@reallorikeefer

THANK YOU!

Get my 7 Tips,
https://www.lorikeefer.com/7tips7posts

Dr. Amba Ann Dryg-Tobin

ANGEL WINGS TO GAIN PERSPECTIVE

For some of us we have magical memories. Magical in that the memories are not exactly as things really happened. We put our own filters on them. If we witnessed a car accident, each one of us would tell the police officer what we saw. Each account of the accident would be a little or very different depending on each person's filters.

Filters come from our past experiences and the stories we have come to believe are true in our minds. Our minds can carry a perspective that led to a belief. Interesting enough, if we shift our perspective, we may find that we change our belief in some way.

For example, when I left Des Moines, Iowa, as an 18-year-old to visit Europe, my perspective was that I was a talented singer, but I would probably never live in Europe as a jazz singer. Once I was there, and singing Billie Holiday tunes solo on the streets, I met musicians. One thing led to another, and nine years passed with me singing in the Netherlands, France, Germany, Belgium, Switzerland, Italy and even Turkey. I didn't believe it could be done until I did it, then my perspective changed as the experiences I had changed my filters.

Coming back to the States was not my idea. My mother was ill and I had to come back. That was 1994 and she died in 1996. By that time, I was living in San Francisco. I remember my good friend and landlord; Steve drove me over the golden gate bridge as the sun was setting and all the oranges and yellows were so beautiful. We sat on the Marin Headlands overlooking the ocean to the right and the bridge on our left. The purples and reds joined the oranges and the yellows as if something extra beautiful was happening in the universe. Yet, something inside me was dying. My mother was brain dead, but still alive. And I was to fly to Iowa the next day. Steve gave me a small rosary to take on the plane.

I remember my perspective at the time in 1996 was that I was losing my mother and that I was being robbed of time with her. My belief at that time was that I would not survive this pain in my chest. It was March and I was sitting on the plane looking over the Mountains over Colorado as the same sun that had set was rising again. I held the rosary in my hand and prayed for mercy from this pain. The plane was coming closer to Denver for us to change planes and I was starting to see the dark reds turn pink-like the roses that my mother grew-- as we came thru the clouds and we started to see the mountains more clearly. I felt my mother's hand on mine. I smelled her face and hair. I knew she was with me.

Before I left the plane, my perspective and belief changed. I knew she would always be with me if I asked for her help, her guidance and her love. The rest of the trip at all times I could feel her just over my shoulder letting me know I could trust she was still there- just not in the physical form any longer. My older sister and brothers did not have the same beliefs as I had. My oldest brother, Alan, really did not take it well. He took her roses, dug them up and took them to Illinois where he lived. He was very close to her.

When I lived in Europe, my mother would send me letters and I would send her postcards. She had saved them all. Our thoughts are leading our perspective. My thoughts at the time were that life could never take such a sharp turn, because I had never experienced death.

That year I had met my first husband. We got married seven months after my mother left her body. I got pregnant and lost the baby that same year as well. I went into depression and despair. I later learned in traditional Chinese medicine, that sadness and grief related to the lungs. Depression or despair related to the heart.

My heart felt like it could not take anymore. Until you have had the experience of a death of a child, you cannot know the perspective or the beliefs you start to have. I appreciate the lessons and wisdom that I gained from that time, and as I tell my clients, its hard to see the challenges as gifts when you are in the thick of it.

My motto is *Every Challenge Is A Gift To Grow And Evolve.* Or that's what I tell people now. To me, and to clients and friends who know me already, my motto is *Every Challenge Is A Gift To Grow And Evolve Closer To God.* Closer to our highest good. Our reason to be here now at this time.

PERSPECTIVES CHANGE OUR BELIEFS

My father had dementia, and I moved him into the home I shared with my second husband. It was a whole new set of challenges and gifts to grow and from which to evolve. I almost lost my husband and my daughters got to see another side of me. My first two grandsons got to know my father and they were the brightest part of his last dark days.

My belief is that every loved one who dies becomes angels whom we know by name. They become entities we can ask for help at any time. I asked for help from my mother. She guided me to the City College of San Francisco to study positive psychology with Dr. Robert Lutz, film production with Caroline Blair and Child Development with Nina Mogar. Nina Mogar encouraged me to study child psychology at San Francisco State University where I got to minor in Holistic Health. Studying Biofeedback with Erik Pepper, Art as Healing with Dr. Michael R. Saso and Autogenic Meditation with Ken Burrows- I learned the power of our thoughts to create change in the physical body thru guided meditation and art. I learned during my psychology internship at Mount Zion University of California San Francisco Cancer Center that I wanted to work with cancer patients using these integrative therapies that I was learning. I could feel nudges from my mother at every corner.

The beliefs had changed greatly as each step I took in my education changed as I took a class called Chinese Perspectives of Holistic Health from acupuncturist Cynthia Chang. She showed us a video of Medical Qigong

Therapy done in China. I immediately recognized what they were doing what I had seen in dreams and in almost all the photos of me that I had. Hands out and open and outstretched. My dance club days always I danced with my hands. When I sang – like with sound healing in Medical Qigong where I helped change the vibration in the room shifting the way people felt.

I knew this was my path. I studied with the Supreme Science Qigong Foundation in Berkeley and later in Florida where I met Wim Hoff. I was trained in Tummo Meditation by Wim, which he now calls the Wim Hoff Method. *You can see Wim on the second season of Gwenyth Paltrow's THE GOOP LAB.

The smell of sugar cookies let me know my mother was there with me. She led me to a Daoist Gathering Conference where the keynote speaker was a very funny and wise man named Professor Dr. Jerry Alan Johnson. He came out of retirement to teach his daughter and 100 other students Medical Qigong Therapy. Later I finished my Doctor of Medical Qigong Therapy with the 54 of us who made it through the very intense program. He would say that, "You Can't Heal What You Don't Feel."

All 54 of us would feel every emotion and express it in a healthy way and go through what he called Ego Deaths. Later, with other teachers I learned that we don't have to suffer to learn valuable lessons. Even the challenges like loosing loved ones does not have to be painful when we understand that God, Source, Divine or however a person calls our higher power.... created a veil of fear around death. Because if we were not afraid of death, we would all end our lives because the other side of the physical body is so much bliss and peace.

Being the light in every room, the lovely, the highest vibration possible is a gift to everyone around us. Having the experiences of death or any challenges we can receive the lessons and transform the uncomfortable emotions into our standing in a higher place with views and perspectives closer to our highest good. Experiences change our perspectives. Perspectives change our beliefs. Free will is sacred. We can choose to take a few steps up to have our highest good perspective. From here we can believer something new about our stories and change our filters of how we see life.

Simple Tools Simplified:

Inhale Innate Virtues and Exhale Acquired Emotions.

To the Heart – inhale Joy, Tranquility and Order
- exhale honoring and letting of any anxiety, nervousness and expectations not met

To the Spleen – inhale Trust, Openness and Sincerity
- exhale honoring and letting go of any worry and overthinking

To the Lungs - inhale Courage, Integrity and Dignity
- exhale honoring and letting go of sadness, grief, shame and guilt

To the Kidneys – inhale Self-Confidence, Inner
Strength and Wisdom
-   exhale honoring and letting go fear and loneliness

To the Liver – inhale Compassion, Kindness and
Patience
-   exhale honoring and letting go of anger, frustration
    and impatience

The most important part of our beliefs and
perspectives of things in our lives is that they in fact bring
about our experiences. Not the other way round.

ACKNOWLEDGEMENTS

Thankful for my family who raised me and who surround me now. In life and death they are all angels who share love with me.

ABOUT AUTHOR

Dr. Amba is the Qigong Lady, a Doctor of Medical Qigong Therapy. She is an author, speaker, teacher and jazz singer. Her life is to be in service with the goal of helping achieve World Peace though more and more individuals feeling inner peace and rippling it out to the World. She is a wife, mother, grandmother and works online and in person with one to 1000 clients at a time. You can find her in Wisconsin, California and all places speaking and teaching. More info at www.sitwellness.com

ABOUT MY BUSINESS

Dr. Amba works with women who have goals of optimal health during times of stress. From Cancer to Fertility she helps all physical, mental and spiritual health disharmonies. She works online for most programs and in person for small and large groups in teaching and in group Medical Qigong Therapy. She incorporates Yoga, Qigong, and Resistance training in her programs as a certified Yoga teacher and Qigong instructor and workshop facilitator. Group Medical Qigong Therapy of 8 to 40 persons in person and 40 to 1000 in online and stadium sessions is a healing art form that has been said to have, "felt like she was working with only me"

Website
www.sitwellness.com

Facebook Personal Page
www.fb.com/amba.tobin

Instagram
https://www.instagram.com/dr.amba_ann_dryg/

THANK YOU OFFER!

Can connect with me for one free session to experience what Medical Qigong Therapy is all about-if you Mention the Book- Expiring in the end of 12/31/22 and You can join any program in the first 6 months of 2022 with no charge with the mention of this book also.

Carol Denise Ward

BREAKING TO BETTER

It is in our breaking that we discover our true strength and are able to grow stronger and ultimately a better version of ourselves.

"Joe, Joe," my pulse is racing, the room is spinning, and my ears are ringing. I want to throw up and run away, hide, pass out. The beeping and flashing of the monitors and the sounds of nurses in the hallway have all faded away. I only hear her tiny voice that is calling out to the heavens. I remember that this is what the hospice nurses had said would happen. That it is a sign of her final passage, but I'm not ready! I can't see straight, but I know that I can help her one last time. I can give her permission to move on. I have to tell her it's ok to go.

"Is it Joe Day?" I ask. "Yes," she whispers. With tears welling and an excruciating pain surging through my entire body, I manage to hold the emotions back long enough to give her one last gift. "It's okay, mom, you can go with Joe; he'll guide your way. We'll be alright, mom. I love you."

The tears begin streaming down my face. The heat and nausea is rising up in me, making my head want to explode. I can't catch my breath. I flee from the room, trying to run from the pain in my heart. My whole world is shattering, my mother is dying tonight, and I can't do anything to change that. How is it possible? She's only 50 years old and hasn't had nearly enough time on this earth. I'm not ready to lose her; I'm not ready to navigate life without her. We have so much more to do together; I have so many questions I haven't asked. I need her to be there for me. At 24 years old, I am too young to be without my mother, my amazing friend, my strength, my number 1 supporter.

With my heartbreaking, looking and feeling like I've been on the losing end of a heavyweight fight, I race down the hallway in a blur. After nine years of fighting off the cancer, my mother can no longer fight, and I cannot heal her. I cannot give her hope. I can only give her my blessing. This time it is too much for her body to endure, and it isn't God's plan to let her suffer any longer, so I have to let her go.

I stumble into the waiting room, unable to speak. My four siblings are there, taking a break from the vigil we have been holding the last few weeks for our mother. Witnessing her deterioration and feeling helpless. I see my sister Beth first; she can tell I've finally reached my breaking point. She understands her baby sister, knows that I never lose control, never allow this level of emotion out. I never let anyone see my pain. Then, somewhere in the fog, I hear her say, "Hey guys! This is serious; Carol has never lost it before!"

As they race in to see her, I sit alone, praying that this is a nightmare I'll wake up from and the pain will go away. It isn't.

So, one by one, each of my siblings say one last goodbye to our mother, giving her permission to pass on and leave us behind in this world. And just like that, we release our mother to be with her angels...

We all have our challenges in this life, our times of breaking; it's how we find our way through them that shapes who we are. Some choose to let it break them, and they spend an eternity reliving the pain, grieving their loss, and never moving forward. Others choose to let it define them, and they wear it like a badge for the world to see what they've endured. They bring it up at every opportunity and create legacies of the pain. And then there is the group I consider myself to be a part of; I choose to find the beauty in the darkness and the lessons in each challenge I face. In each tragedy, I find an opportunity for growth and a possible opening for a new beginning, a new path to forge, a new direction to explore.

I have had many opportunities to "grow" in my life. I have felt the deep, gut-wrenching pain of breaking where I can't breathe, I can't think, my world is crashing in, many times along my path, and each time I have learned and grown. With each **crack,** there is a light, an opportunity, a way out. It is painful, but each crack reveals a new opening, a new beginning. Always learning, always growing. Becoming a better version of me.

My mother's death was the first excruciating **Break** for me.

Mom had been sick a long time. When I was 16, she was diagnosed with breast cancer. That was when the first **Crack** of that excruciating **Break** came. My mother struggled to stay positive and strong for nine long years as the disease kept rearing its ugly head and taking pieces of her away. First, it was her breast, causing her to struggle with her femininity. Next, it took her voice when the cancer traveled to her vocal cords and tried to silence her fierce strength. Lastly, the disease morphed into her bones, destroying her independence and breaking her spirit.

This woman that raised me and shaped me was outrageously strong and courageous. She also had a gypsy spirit. One of her greatest passions was traveling and exploring the country on a shoestring. She had been planning a six-week cross-country camping trip when she was told that she had breast cancer and would need to start chemo treatments right away. And so like no other sane person would do, she said ok, but I'm still going to take this trip, and we're going to map out where I'll be when I need to have a treatment, and you're going to find hospitals and set up the appointments in those cities. I can only imagine how stunned the doctors were back in 1977 when this 5'4", 42- year-old woman told them how it was going to happen. But, they could see her intense passion and conviction and knew that their only option was to work with her, and they gave her the best hospitals across the country that fit her schedule. Was she stubborn? Um, YES! Was she strong? Hell YES!!

We took off in July of 1977 and started that 6-week trip driving over 10,000 miles, setting up the tent trailer in campgrounds everywhere we went, and as planned, on her chemo days, we would arrive at the designated hospital where she would jump out of the car, check-in for her infusion and a few hours later emerge from the hospital and we'd be back on the road. We stuck by her rigid plan and never deterred from it. We pulled over for her to be sick until she gathered her strength, then we would motor on once more.

This was normal in my world. No one ever questioned my mother, and she never asked for sympathy or exceptions. I didn't see her as a superhuman, outrageously strong-willed, and intensely resilient. She would allow nothing to stand in her way, but to me, it was just mom being mom. What I also didn't realize was that this strength was shaping me... I was witnessing firsthand the power of a positive mindset, devoted prayer, and formidable determination.

Much of our healing comes from within, and we have the ability to heal both ourselves and others. Her journey is one great example of this. My mother recovered from the breast cancer and was declared cancer-free for five solid years!

My senior year in college was very busy studying, having fun, and planning my upcoming wedding. Nevertheless, I would call home each week and talk to my mother. As the school year went on, I noticed she seemed to have a constant cold, and that's where the next **Crack** came. As I was graduating from college, my mother's cancer had returned. This time it tried to quiet her mighty voice. She had become hoarse from the growth on her vocal cords, and many days her voice was barely a whisper.

But as you can imagine, her immense strength, stubbornness, and determination kicked into high gear as she cheered me on through my college graduation, not telling me about the return of the disease until after my big day was over. She was there with my father and family, rooting for me as I crossed that stage and received the first college diploma of my siblings. It was a huge moment for me, and she made it so special. (Being the youngest of 5 kids, it wasn't often I felt special.)

Immediately after graduation, I learned about the return of her cancer and saw her incredible spirit, determined to beat this too! She had a "quick" surgery, and her doctors said that she would probably have another 5-10 years. This meant nothing to her. She was determined to beat this the same way she'd beaten the previous bout, and her mind was set hard on that goal. Encouraging her and remaining positive was how I was able to help in her battle.

I began to prepare for my wedding that was less than five months away. Again, she kept her treatments private, never letting them interfere with her plans. As we shopped for the wedding, people would hear her whisper of a voice and invariably ask if she had a cold or wasn't feeling well, and she would generally respond that yes, it was a little laryngitis and leave it at that. Her level of "Suck It Up Buttercup" was incredible! Keeping her mindset positive and believing that "this too shall pass." Every day I would watch her smile offer the same polite response to people, never revealing her condition and concerns.

I had learned from her to keep my troubles to myself, and God forbid, never ask for help. I have to admit that it may not have been the best lesson to learn. But, it is one I have begun to unravel as I become more aware that the only way to form true connections and to heal yourself is by letting others in, allowing them to see your pain along with your joy. Hiding our pain only leads to more disease. So to heal, we must be vulnerable.

After my wedding, my husband and I moved to Massachusetts to our new home. I was now 6 hours from my parents and made a point of calling home every week to check in with my mom. I'd offer encouragement, telling her that her voice was sounding stronger, and that meant the treatments must be working. Finally, one day she let down her stoic guard and said, "Do you really think so? It means a lot to me that you can hear the improvements in my voice." It gave her hope and encouragement to keep powering through, to keep healing. I hadn't realized how much my words meant to her until that moment. The power of a kind word, a vote of confidence, and unconditional love can help push someone through their darkest times. These words of encouragement were my mother's lifeline for healing; my strength and belief in her became her beacon of hope. I was helping to heal her through my words. As the months progressed, I made sure that I always gave her the words she needed to hear. At 22, I was becoming my mother's healer.

"People will forget what you said, people will forget what you did, but people will never forget how you made them feel."
— *Maya Angelou*

Once again, my mother had found the strength to heal her disease and go on with her life as planned. She was so resilient and determined to get the most out of every moment of her life. My world was good once more, and I felt like I could breathe again.

The third giant **Crack** in that excruciating **Break** came a few years later as I settled into a job and married life. On my weekly phone call on a bright day in August 1984, I heard, "I have a pain in my hip that I'm going to go get checked out. " My heart sank. My mother had to have been in intense pain for her to even mention it let alone go get it checked out. I tried to convince myself that it was just a pull or muscle strain. But I had a horrible gut feeling about the results. When we talked the following week, she confirmed the worst. The cancer had returned. I could hear in her voice the defeat, the lack of fight, the sheer exhaustion that this gave her. She wasn't up for this fight, and I felt the same exhaustion. As she was experiencing her new pain, I was experiencing similar pain. Although mine resulted from a water skiing accident, they were the same neck, back, and hip trouble she was experiencing.

My mother had fought off the cancer twice, but this time it had made her crumble. Her body could no longer physically support her in this realm and was just waiting for her soul to let go. All my siblings had come in from around the country and were with her in those last few days. We visited, watched, and waited. My father kept constant vigilance in the corner of her room, sitting in a chair, watching and praying. Then, after we had said our goodbyes to her and gone home that final night, he was there alone with her and our minister until she passed — the ever-loving, ever-loyal partner who I never saw cry until she was gone.

CHANGED FOREVER

When the matriarch of your family passes, the family is forever changed. My mother was the superglue of our family. Her drive and determination to keep us all connected as a family were paramount to anything else in her life. With my siblings being all over the country, it had been a full-time job for her to check in on everyone and update each of us on what the others were doing and to orchestrate getting everyone home for family gatherings. Connection, Connection, Connection. She loved us all fiercely but rarely showed it outwardly. We were not a demonstrative family when it came to emotions. But I still knew that I was definitely her favorite!!

Losing my mother broke my heart and left me feeling so guilty that I had given up on her. Not being able to heal her has haunted me. Would things have been different if I hadn't felt so exhausted by her last illness? I'll never know for sure, but I am grateful that I was able to give her the gift of peace. We are not designed to live forever, so learning to be at peace with our path is also part of our healing.

As the decades passed, I found myself trying to be the superglue that my mother had once been—and trying hard to stay connected to everyone. I made the drive to NY for everyone's big moments because I wanted to be a part of everyone's lives, and I wanted to help heal the family the only way I knew how. Love, connection, and presence. Without my mother to guide me, I did my best to assume her position and maintain the feeling that I was called to heal the family. At times it is so hard. I don't always have the words to explain to my husband why it's so important to me to always run and help them no matter what they ask for. I ache to have their acceptance and for them all to love one another, forgive each other, and to remember that family should always come first. That we can learn from our errors and forgive each other so that we can all heal, that our wounds can heal with love.

As I navigated my way through adulthood, I had signs of my intuition growing stronger. But listening to it was a challenge! I began seeing signs that the Universe was sending me messages. I would drive by a certain spot and feel the energy exploding from it. I knew that there was one particular spot along my daily commute that held my mother's energy. Every day it would catch my attention. No matter what I was thinking, a vision of her would pop into my head, and I noticed that it was at the same exact spot every time. I would just breathe in her essence. I had no words or explanation for it back then, but I felt it as some type of sacred ground that I was continually drawn to.

Intuition was both tough and a gift in the business world. Being so logical in my careers of Accounting and IT, quantifying things was the expected path so going on my "gut" was not always the easiest thing to explain. One place I always excelled was in the software world. I had numerous opportunities to test new software for bugs and invariably would find some really crazy issues. I could simply dive into one scenario and uncover bugs within a few moments. I called it a gift for finding programming errors, but now I know my intuition guided me to those specific areas.

I began learning and exploring intuition, universal energy, and spirit guidance. At some level, I believed in it, and at other times I had trouble believing. It isn't an area that is logical but is what my soul was calling for. Each time I had a "tarot card reading" done, I was amazed at its accuracy and the insights offered. I had a level of respect and awe for people who practiced mediumship and other modalities. I knew that there were messages that I needed to hear and was trying to listen to my own instincts. Learning and growing and praying for guidance.

The world is looking pretty good; my career and personal life are doing well and then...**Crack**!

It was midnight; the phone was ringing. As they say, no one calls with good news late at night. The call was from my oldest sister. She told me that my sister Beth was in the hospital in Poughkeepsie, NY, a 3-hour ride from me. This was her 3rd or 4th ambulance ride in the last six months for what was believed to be asthma attacks. Each time, she had been rushed to the hospital, given breathing treatments, and sent home. This time was different. I could feel the urgency in my sister's voice. Beth was my best friend, and I needed her to be ok. I was a complete wreck on the inside but needed to keep it together for all of us. It was probably the most frightening ride of my life on dark, slick, snowy unfamiliar roads. I felt sick to my stomach and was terrified of what this could be. Finally, I arrived at the hospital with her twin daughters that had been visiting me. We were utterly exhausted but wired from adrenaline.

She was very sick and required open heart surgery. Anxiously waiting through the surgery and recovery room, the wait seemed too long. They weren't letting us see her, there were no explanations, and it was getting late. I was getting worried that something was wrong. Finally, we were allowed to see her even though she still wasn't awake. We held her hands, touched her arm and her face, told her we loved her, and waited. Then came a sign from above, a special Jamaican nurse had arrived for her. I knew that she would be ok. (I had been rescued before by mysteriously appearing Jamaican women.)

When it was time for Beth to be released from the hospital, my husband and I offered our home as her convalescence spot. We have a quiet, peaceful home and had the resources to allow her to recover. Our home is a healing space.

By day she would sit in my "Healing" chair. (It was where I had put a number of people over the years that had one ailment or another because it seems to be just right for everyone, so I had begun calling it the "Healing" chair without even realizing that I was a healer myself.) By night she slept soundly in the make-shift bedroom we had created in our living room.

My sister's recovery required round-the-clock care, so we had a revolving door of family and friends staying with us to help her recover. On the rare occasion she was alone; I had a list of people I could call to check on her if needed. The peace of mind that comes from knowing people have your back when you're in a crisis is one thing that helped keep me sane. The other thing was the workouts I had grown accustomed to. My trainer was fun, caring, and gifted in fixing people's bodies which in turn fixed minds. I knew I needed to take care of myself in order to have the energy to take care of others. That's what my workouts with my trainer did for me.

After ten weeks at my home, we felt Beth was ready to make the 6-hour ride home to finish her recovery. So in late May, Beth and I made the trek back to NY, settled her in, and I returned to Massachusetts to pick up my life. I had devoted my time and energy to keeping my sister safe and allowing her the space and the love to help her heal both physically and emotionally. Now it was my turn. I was tired and needed to recharge fully.

My recharge was short-lived...

Just five weeks later and...**Crack**! Another phone call, another crisis to pull me into the caretaker, rescuer, connector avenue that I knew only too well. My brother called from TX. He was in the hospital, waiting for test results. (Are you kidding me?!?) I felt sick and wanted this to be a false alarm. He gave me a run-down of his health over the past two years and how he had finally consented to getting checked out by a doctor. I called my sisters, and we all started theorizing on the different outcomes and praying for a simple answer with a positive outcome... Not this time. I felt like I had been punched in the gut with the next update. He had stage 4 lung cancer and only a short time to live without treatment and only a few months more with treatment. CRAP!!!!!! This can't be happening. Now, what do we do???

Out of all my siblings, my brother is the one I knew the least. He had moved to TX when I was in high school and only came back home to NY a handful of times over the next 30 years. His youngest was only three months old the only time I met her, and was now a very shy 14-year-old with a very sick dad. I was determined to get to know them all and show them that they had family that loved them and that they could count on. I wanted so badly for this nightmare to go away and for everyone to be healthy and whole. I wanted more time to build back relationships and wipe away the years of distance. I just wanted more!

I began making trips to Texas to reconnect my brother's family to me. My heart was full and breaking all at the same time. I remember wanting to reach out and lay my hands on my brother's arm and let him know he would be okay. Somewhere deep inside me, I felt like I could heal him or take away his pain if I would just touch him. I still wish I had followed through with that urge. At the time, I had no idea what power there is in a healing touch.

As my sister and I were getting ready to go home from my first trip, my brother told us that his wife and kids had been curious about why we would come and what we would do while we were there. After all, we had never been to Austin the entire 30 years he had lived there. He explained, "These are the Power Sisters! They're going to come in, assess the situation, make some adjustments, and then head back home." Seriously?!?! I guess he knew us better than I thought. So... We are the **POWER SISTERS**. I LOVE that title, and I remember that day fondly.

Over the next few months, my Power Sister and I lived up to our new titles. We took turns escorting our father and other two sisters to Texas to reconnect with my brother and his family. My heart was wide open with love and connecting to each and every one of them. I prayed that they all realized that I would always be there for them. I felt that the family was healing.

Every trip to Austin was both unique and special. The last time I saw my brother was at his oldest son's wedding. Exactly one year after my brother's diagnosis, I escorted my 80-year-old father and stepmother down to Texas for the event (my father had remarried just as my mother wanted). My brother had managed to squeeze one more year of life out of his body and was able to attend his oldest son's wedding. What an incredible show of strong will, determination, and faith this had been. He fought hard to see that day and be a part of his son's wedding.

Sadly, my brother began to decline quickly after the wedding and passed seven weeks later. I was never able to lay my hands on him in the way I had envisioned. I didn't feel comfortable just reaching out and touching him. We had not been brought up to hug or touch, so I never found a way to be that close to him physically. I barely hugged anyone at that point of my life. I was so shut down to my emotions that I wasn't aware of how much I needed hugs and human touch. I always felt awkward and didn't understand that I was being called to be an energy healer.

Despite not being able to heal my brother physically, I was able to heal his spirit and give his soul peace in his final days. I am learning that healing comes in many forms, and we all have our own unique gifts to heal.

Pennies from heaven...

I found that saying goodbye only signaled that I could no longer talk to his physical being. My brother was a gifted soul and helped me keep the promises I had made to him for a long time. After he passed, he would "contact me." I would see pennies in the oddest places, and I knew it was a sign from him that one of his children or his wife needed something. So, I would pause, breathe in the message, and call his family. Invariably, there was an issue that needed some intervention, and I was happy to be the conduit and help them any way I could. After all, a promise is a promise! Pennies from heaven is a real thing.

I have learned that loss is such an individual experience. As I reflect on the years since my brother passed, I can see how each person, each child, wife, sister, father, friend reacted differently, uniquely. Our relationships carry so many levels and we all need to accept the ways each person manages that loss. There is no right or wrong, there is only different. Just like a snowflake, there is a uniqueness to each of us and to the relationships we develop.

Just do it...

After losing a sibling and nearly losing another, I learned to act on my crazy ideas. You never know what life has in store for you, so learning to listen to that voice within will open you up for some incredible experiences. So in 2010, I acted on my crazy! I had won travel vouchers at our company Christmas party, and I realized that with some shifting and reallocating... I could pull off a first-time ever Sisters' trip, and what better place to do that in but Aruba!

What a cool idea!!! I didn't want to second guess myself or waste any time putting this together because if my sisters needed passports, they needed as much time as possible to get them, and I just wanted to make it happen now. And besides, you never know when the next Crack in our lives will come.

So, on my ride home from the office party, I jumped on the phone and talked to each of my three sisters about a trip to Aruba. Yes, they all thought I was crazy, but they know better than to mess with my crazy. I was flying high when I got home and couldn't wait to start booking it. I can still feel my heart pumping wildly just thinking about that day, hearing the excitement in each of my sisters as they told me I was nuts, but of course, they would go. I love them all so much, and being together was all I wanted to do. I have always looked for those signs from the Universe, and my brother's death seemed to have strengthened my intuition. It also gave me a stronger drive to act on them even if they seemed crazy. Some of my best memories are of moments like this.

So, six weeks later, there we were..... Sitting on the warm Aruba sand, listening to the waves flow in and out, feeling the brilliantly warm sun on our skin and feeling the ever present warm breeze across our bodies. Five glorious days of giving ourselves the best medicine possible. We bobbed around in the surf, reminiscing, dreaming, and recharging our souls. We didn't know then that it would be our only sisters' trip for the four of us.

At the end of the gloriously rejuvenating week, we all headed in our different directions, back to our lives. My sisters returned to their homes and businesses in NY, and I returned to my home and my job in MA.

Give Till It Hurts...

My work has been a huge part of who I am, or so I always thought. It has certainly impacted, guided, developed, and taught me countless lessons for good and bad, but happily, it isn't what has ultimately defined me. I have a BS in Business Administration and Accounting. I spent 30 years being a corporate professional, managing and directing people and processes. I've had staff and management responsibilities from my very first job, and I loved most of it...until I didn't. When my job fit into my life it was great. When it wanted to BE my life it wasn't great. When it wanted me to give it my life, it needed to go.

I am a strong, resilient and ingenious woman. I'm also kind, loving, and extremely compassionate. When I would stand up for myself, I was generally terrified. It was both the scariest and the best feeling ever. But, when I let people walk all over me and try to push me into a corner, it was painful and soul-crushing, and unbelievably frustrating. A corporate career can give you every range of emotion, and it can destroy you if you let it.

I loved working. I loved accomplishing things and creating the impossible. Looking back, I realize that some of the solutions I designed during my career were probably channeled. They were brilliant moments that I had no idea how to recreate. It was my magic. I was willing to work long days, occasional weekends, and carry a mobile device 24/7 once they became a thing. But, when it was vacation time, I made sure I went away. My recharge time was non-negotiable regardless of what was falling down around me at work. I understood that in order to give so completely, I needed to rest and recharge on my vacations. I may be in the minority, but I know that unless you work in a life or death industry, whatever problem arises can wait, or can be solved by another without you, so I never canceled or cut short a vacation.

Being enslaved to a company was not my plan for eternity. I knew that I needed freedom to find what the Universe was calling me to do. It had been a regular feeling over the last 20+ years that there was something more. When it was time to move on, I found myself literally pacing like a caged animal. I would go for walks to alleviate the anxiousness. One day, I found myself 2 miles from the office before I realized where I was. The time to move on was upon me once more. This company had become a prison to me, and I no longer felt energized by my accomplishments.

A few years before leaving my corporate life, I started dreaming of what my life would look like if I went a different route. I saw myself traveling around visiting clients, making my own schedule, and working with people I wanted to be around. I could see it, I could feel it, I could taste it! This vision became so regular and so real that I began to believe that I could have that life. I knew that it would feel amazing to be that free and independent. I needed to find the path that would be for me and not for someone else's dream.

I left my last corporate job after 12 years, choosing to walk away from a great salary, decent benefits, and some very good friends. But, this time I chose **ME**! I chose my health, and I chose my heart, my dignity, and my sanity. I chose My dream.

They say... If you dream it, you can live it. Just let the Universe know you're serious.

It's beautiful how the Universe rewards you for making tough decisions. After months of discussions with my husband about how truly awful my work environment had become and that even attempting to look for something else while feeling so beat up was not an option, we agreed that I would resign. Decision made, resignation letter started. The very next morning, not even 12 hours after making the decision and putting pen to paper, I had an email asking me to consider a position at a company that was looking to expand. I kid you not; it happened that quickly! This offer was from a woman I had become friends with while working on the board of a not for profit group. We had worked well together for many years, and she appreciated all the skills I brought to the table. (It's so nice to be recognized and appreciated for who you are.) I responded that she had impeccable timing and was definitely interested in the conversation. **OMG**!!! Now I could breathe a giant sigh of relief. I had a safety net, and I was valued. This was all I needed to finish the resignation process and put this toxic chapter to bed.

How many lessons did I need to learn from this? I am worthy? I will be ok? When you make room, something better comes along? Yes, Yes, and Yes!

WOW, the confidence that comes from being sought out by someone you respect is incredible. Knowing that they recognize your value and see you as an asset in their vision is truly amazing. Not to mention the comfort of having a safety net.

I finished the resignation, cleaned out my office, and picked the right day to deliver the news. I wanted everything to be wrapped up nicely before actually handing in my resignation. So I went down my checklist one last time.

> New managers on board to take care of my staff and systems...*Check.*

> Brain dump to the project team of every decision, every program, every process created and documented over the last 12 years... *Check.*

> Personal items taken home from my office... *Check.*

> Contacts loaded to my personal database... *Check.*

> Safety net in place...... *Check*

> Goodbyes...Sadly, no check.

As I went to pick up the last of my things in my office, I took a look around the giant room, and I already saw myself as an outsider looking in. Like a hazy movie winding down and the sound cutting out with just a blur of activity going by, then Click..... my big heavy office door latches and locks one last time. I'm floating in a fog, walking back to HR to drop off my key. My eyes are looking downward, afraid that if I look at anyone, I'm going crumble to the ground and cry. I don't want anyone to see me Crack or watch me Break. I drop the key, and thankfully no one is there to see me. I turn and walk towards the elevator; my heart is beating so hard I can taste it—only 50 more feet to the elevator. I'm almost free. I'll be ok if I can get on the elevator in one piece. It's all I can do to not fall to the floor as I make my way around the corner. My knees are shaking. Two colleagues are walking by, deep in conversation. They look up, see my computer bag in hand, my coat on, and joke about me leaving early. I smile somehow and say, yeah, something like that. And then BAM! The shopping bag I was carrying hit my leg, and my Staples Easy Button went off saying, **"That Was Easy"**! I burst out laughing, grateful for the release of the tension that had been building like a pressure cooker all day and grateful for the sign that I was definitely doing the right thing. Thank you, Universe! I was now ready to peek through the Crack in me that this had created and to see the light to dance my way into a new life, a new chapter, a new opportunity, and a new me! One step closer to taking me back. The me I never knew was hiding. I was listening to my heart and following my intuition.

Money isn't everything...

When you consider your options in life, consider more than just the price tag. My "savior," that asked me to help her grow her company, did not have deep pockets, but she had an enormous heart, and that was what I wanted to work with. I was done working in an environment of every person for themselves and thrilled to be working with someone that valued and respected me. What a joy to be on my new path, helping her grow her practice and putting processes in place for sustained growth. Really?

Well, it was fun and new and freeing to be working from home, checking in remotely, and learning a new way of life. It gave me a great reason to set up a real home office with a desk, file cabinet, and a real office chair! It was so silly, but I really enjoyed setting up my very own office. It also gave me time to regroup and recover from the physical and emotional toll my last job had taken on me. It was time to figure out some good habits for working at home. This job was a blank canvas. These were all good things and exciting things, so what was missing? People!!! I craved people and relationships, and connection. My soul needed the energy of other people. My friends recognized this quicker than I did. They literally told me one day, "Girl, you need to get out of that house!" After 30 years of being accountable to an office and office hours and the structure of a corporate job, I hadn't realized just how accustomed I'd become to daily interactions and how much I now missed that.

My friends proceeded to drag me to my first networking event. My first what? What's a networking event? I had no idea what this was, but they were so right.

I definitely needed this. I instantly knew that being around energetic people boosted my energy and really filled me up. I began learning about entrepreneurship and network marketing, and sales and other networking groups and chambers of commerce, and my head was spinning! I learned about so many crazy products, services, business models, and people. Wow, corporate life is so boring and limiting compared to this group that was filled with people brave enough to follow their passions, scrape for customers and build their dreams. They weren't afraid of how hard it was or how different it was; they believed they could do it, and they made you believe in them. It was a whole other economy I never knew existed, and I was so grateful for this introduction. My soul was waking up and cheering me on. I was finding my people. I was finding me! I hadn't realized that I had spent decades just going through the motions, doing my job, and never really connecting with anyone. I was lonely; I didn't have a tribe. I didn't have a safe place to be me and feed my soul. I was waking up and seeing how empty I was spiritually.

Shift...

Fast forward a year, I was getting itchy again about working for someone else even though I had a lot of freedom. I was ready to try something on my own... Just as I was getting ready to give it a try, my current work was winding down, and we chose to lay me off. She really didn't need me anymore and I was ready to fly so it was a win, win for both of us. Thank you once again, Universe, for hearing my voice and opening the door for me. The twists and turns of our lives force us to be creative, flexible and invite us to be open to opportunities as they arise. And then along the way, when you open your mind and your heart, you begin to find you.

As I immersed myself into this new commerce of the direct sales and network marketing arena, phrases like "find your big why" or "the why that makes you cry" became my new normal, along with learning my "elevator pitch" and finding my "brand." And OMG, this was not an easy path. I didn't know what I didn't know. Some days I just wanted to curl up in a corner and hide or cry, but then I would pull myself together, adjust my mindset, raise my vibration and head out to meet someone for coffee or attend a networking event. I had so much to learn. I kept my eyes, ears, and mind open and just kept pushing forward. The new relationships I was building were so fun and different. I was learning and growing, and uncovering me. I was happy. My soul was waking up.

The business I chose to pursue was the result of that very first networking event my friends had dragged me to. I had met a woman there who introduced me to a simple greeting card concept that would change me forever. It taught me about gratitude and gave me a vehicle to express that gratitude, and it fed my need to be creative.

This greeting card business opened my heart in ways I never knew were possible. It took time for my real voice to emerge, but I send love, joy, and inspiration to people every day and receive so much in return. Touching someone's heart at the precise time they need it is the pure magic I have found.

Remember that dream I was having before leaving my corporate life? The one about freedom and travel and making my own schedule? This work is what I was dreaming of so many years ago. The dreams and visualization that I did had suddenly come together and resulted in what I am doing today. This was the feeling I had been looking for all those years ago. Traveling to meet people that I wanted to meet and the freedom to make my own schedule—feeling free and joyous. The bonus of making people happy has become the most important part of these cards.

It's hard work, but I have met amazing people, forged unimaginable relationships, and learned so much. My soul is learning to speak through this medium, and my ability to listen to my intuition is growing. I believe in the magic that happens when I act on an impulse that comes to me. Learning to not question it but to act on it has taught me how connected we all are in this world. Just lean in and listen. That's where the magic is.

Each experience prepares you for the next.

Personal development books, podcasts, and programs have become part of my daily life. The more I learn, the more I want to learn. My interests are so widespread that I say yes to so many different opportunities that I lose track sometimes. But I am allowing my soul to lead me as I explore the world. I am creating connections and relationships far beyond anything I ever imagined.

Along the way, I have become aware that I am so energized by meeting and talking to people. Hearing people's stories and watching them light up when they tell me what they're passionate about is intoxicating. I have learned to be curious, to listen, and to say yes to new experiences. I am waking up and finding my own passions. Healing is my passion. Finding new ways to impact people is my passion. And I was and am deeply happy about that.

But then there's that next .... **Crack**. The phone rings, it's 9 am, and I can barely understand my niece on the other end. She is hysterically crying and screaming, and I can't console her. It's about her mom, my sister, and best friend, Beth. She's dead. I'm stunned. My heart is breaking into a million pieces, but I need to help my niece. I ask her to hand the phone to whoever is driving, and I gently ask the girl to pull over and try to calm my niece down. I tell her to hug her and don't let go. In my heart, I'm hugging her as well. I was not yet aware that that was possible, but I knew that it was what I wanted so badly.

Once my niece is calmer, I hang up and fall apart. I crumble to the floor sobbing and unable to move. When I take a breath, I call my husband, who is 45 minutes away. How had this happened? Had I given up on her like I had with my mother? Why couldn't I heal her? My soul wanted to scream and comfort her all at the same time. I felt I had let her down. Somewhere along the line, I made myself responsible for healing everyone in my life. It seemed that when I gave up, they died. Why couldn't I stay strong and hold them up? Why did I get depleted and let them pass?

On our way to NY the next day to be with my family, I told my husband I needed to speak at her funeral. I had never done that, and I was terrified of public speaking, but I knew I had to speak. I was listening to my soul and needed to tell her story. How do you sum up 50 years together in just a few short paragraphs? I have no idea.

All I knew was whatever was meant to be said would come out. I trusted the Universe to lead me. When it was my turn, I spoke, my voice was clear and strong, my focus was laser, the words flowed the message was exactly what I had hoped for. I was able to inject some humor into it, which is what Beth always did. I believe I made Beth proud, and I felt good that I didn't let her down. We all do what we must when we're called upon. These are the moments when we grow the most.

I am forever grateful that I acted on my crazy and took my sisters on our one and only sisters' trip. That will always be such a precious memory for me and a huge reminder to follow that voice within me. To trust my intuition.

SPEAKING OF CRAZY

A few years later, a woman showed up at a networking luncheon I was attending. She said that her sole purpose was to find one person to join her spiritual retreat to Scotland. Within 48 hours, I'd registered for the trip, booked my flights, and grilled my father about his father, who had immigrated from Scotland as a young boy. I had no idea who this woman was, who else would be traveling, or what a "spiritual retreat" really was. But I knew deep inside of me that this was a trip I was destined to take.

Scotland was amazing, eye-opening, and just the tip of the iceberg in my spiritual journey. I watched, listened, and followed the other people in the group who had traveled on this woman's journeys before. We meditated (another first for me), we did some ancient rituals on sacred ground (it felt weird, but I was trusting), and we visited some pretty cool places. I began feeling a connection to this group and opening a part of me that I had never explored. It was a curiosity about this level of connection, of knowing and spiritual awareness. And I was finding my tribe.

And so, my journey of trusting my instincts and saying yes to new and interesting opportunities continued. Each new experience brought amazing people into my life. Being open to anything is such an incredible way to live. There is no impossible when you believe in possibilities.

My next spiritual journey was to Peru with the same woman but different travelers. I spent two soul-enriching weeks learning, connecting, and growing. Peru felt like home to me, and I could feel every shift in energy and the intensity of the sacred spaces we were in. The air was so clear, the mountains so high, and the people exuded love. Just being there was like one giant meditation. My soul was finding its voice and its people, people who understood the power of faith, prayer, reverence, and healing.

While on this Peruvian trip, I witnessed the power of intention and deep connection. Our guide took us to his hometown, and we were blessed every day with everything aligning perfectly in our paths. When anything attempted to go awry, we simply stepped back, refocused, and our journey would continue effortlessly. I witnessed torrential rains suddenly ending, jammed crowds opening pathways for us to walk through, and flights being rearranged to allow us a clear and calm terminal amidst a throng of chaotic terminals.

I was feeling my heart open with my fellow journeymen. We were experiencing incredible visions and miracles that were bringing us closer together. This was another group of beautiful souls that I knew would be with me for years to come.

Then **Crack......** Just a few short months after returning from Peru, I found out just how important faith and friends are. Our nephew and his wife gave birth to what is termed as "micropremie" twin boys. What should have been the most precious moments of their lives had turned into a living nightmare. The boys were born at just 25 weeks, 15 weeks early, and under 2 lbs each. Even though we don't have children of our own, my husband and I have 17 nieces and nephews and 29 great-nieces and nephews between us. This was an eye-opening, heart-wrenching first. We prayed, and we prayed, and we prayed. I called upon my friends and fellow spirtualists to send love and healing at each crisis. They all rallied around me and my family.

The boys began to turn a corner. They were still extremely small and had many more challenges ahead of them, but we all took a little breath as the critical moments became fewer over the next several weeks. The power of many is astounding, and the boys had people praying for them and healing them worldwide!! I became a complete believer in the power of healing. The precious boys are three years old now and growing stronger every day.

When you're meant to do something...

Through all of these journeys, a feeling had always been inside me that I wished I could do more for the people in my life. I wished that I could make their pain and suffering go away. So, following my crazy, I said yes to a half-day workshop being given by a man that I had been following for a few years. I'd always found his talks intriguing, and the crystal bowls he played spoke to me at a level I couldn't explain.

And the next thing I knew, I'd signed up for the school he ran.

OMG! It's a healing school?!?

Here I am on my very first day of class, and they tell us that we'll be doing a healing a little later in the day. Say what?!?!? Never in my wildest dreams did I see this coming. Or did I?? Hmmm.......

After the first weekend of class, I called my father, who was 91 at the time and said, "Ok, 40 years ago, mom said you had healing hands. Tell me about that." As he recalled a very vague memory of that experience in his life, I told him about my new school and that it looked like I just might like this and be good at it. Unfortunately, my dad has never done anything with his ability and has nearly forgotten that he had ever been told that he was a healer. I sure could have used a mentor.

I dove in so deep to school that year. I practiced on everyone; I had clients from 16 years old to 80 years old — people from every occupation, and every religious affiliation. But I wasn't a complete woo-woo person and had a very matter-of-fact approach about it. I believe that my experiences in life have all led to this moment. I was exposing the healer in me that had been crying to get out all these years. I now understood my feelings about my brother, mother, and sister. I AM a healer. I have been one my whole life. I now have tools to further develop my abilities and consciously help people.

It may be a twisted journey, but nothing in our lives is ever a mistake. Each obstacle brings new opportunities to learn and grow. Each Crack creates an opening, a light to new opportunities and growth. When we Break, we are not broken. We are letting in the dark and finding the light that is needed to grow.

Each new experience prepares us for something greater. We are ever learning, ever-evolving beings that need one another. Connecting with one another and impacting each other's lives for good is the essence of my soul and yours, too, if you look inside. So, at 61 years old, I find myself stepping into my calling as an energy healer. I am grateful that I was led to the energy healing school so that I could help so many people in this trying time.

We are truly never too old to find out who we are. The key is to lean in and listen. The signs are all around us when we open our eyes and our hearts to being the best version of ourselves. Being able to put it into words and practice has been a gift that I intend to share with as many people as possible.

Each time we Break, we emerge to a Better, stronger, softer version of who we are intended to be.

Dream, Connect, Grow and Be Grateful

ACKNOWLEDGEMENTS

I would like to thank so many people for making this story come to print. I thank my family, my parents, my grandparents, my siblings, my in-laws, my nieces, my nephews and my greats for accepting my uniqueness and allowing me the space to grow. I pray that you always give yourselves and those around you the same grace you have given me. Each of our journeys are unique and we never know what's deep inside of one another. I want to thank my husband David who has been with me most of my life and who always strives to support me in my journey regardless of the twists and turns I throw at him. Whether he understands what I'm doing or not, he is there. His quiet way of loving me through acts of service keeps me going and keeps me grounded. I want to thank my coach Bonnie Surie who has helped me put into action the truths that are hiding within me and for helping me to say them out loud. I want to thank Dorris Burch for allowing me this space to tell my story and find my voice. I also want to Thank Rhys Thomas, the Rhys Thomas Institute and my classmates for guiding me through the treacherous inner growth (often times kicking and screaming!) that has brought me to this place in my life where I can be who I'm meant to be. It has been invaluable and I have needed every one of you to get me here. Thank you God.

ABOUT THE AUTHOR

After 30 years of towing the line as a leader in her corporate positions, Carol has stepped out of the shadows to reveal her true calling and place in the world. She has broken free of the constrictions of traditional roles to become an entrepreneur and healer. Her lifetime of experiences has led Carol to the place she is today. Through pain, sorrow, revelation and hard work she has risen up to be the resilient woman that is admired by those she works with. Carol has a servant heart and aspires to lead the world out of their darkness and into the beautiful souls they are intended to be.

ABOUT MY BUSINESS

CarolDenise.com is a multi layered approach to human kindness and raising the vibration and consciousness of everyone in its path. Utilizing Energy Medicine, Greeting Cards, Coaching and Speaking we are able to work to transform our clients into better versions of their true self by realigning their energetic self and realigning them with their clients, friends and family.

Website
www.caroldenise.com

Facebook Personal Page
https://www.facebook.com/carol.ward.3766

Instagram
https://www.instagram.com/wardinn/

THANK YOU!

As a thank you, I'm offering a complimentary Chakra Balance Session and Mantra Card.

PUBLISHER ACKNOWLEDGMENTS

It takes a village to produce a book, and I am deeply grateful for the creative forces and dedication of every single person who added her or his magic to this one.

This is the eighth book in our Don't Be Invisible Be Fabulous series – and I am deeply honored.

My whole-hearted appreciation starts with the readers and supporters of our first, best-selling book; they inspired the second, third, fourth, fifth, sixth, seventh and now eighth volume. This journey reinforced in my bones how essential it is to tell stories of real-life women triumphing in their lives. Thousands of women saw themselves in those stories, and then they could imagine a way forward in their own lives. So, of course, Volume 8, featuring more stories of hope and inspiration, had to be born!

Heaps of appreciation also go to the fabulous coauthors from our first, second, third, fourth, fifth. sixth and seventh books:

Thank you all!

Don't Be Invisible. Be Fabulous!

LEARN MORE

SOCIAL MEDIA

Website
TheFabFactor.com

Message me on FB Messenger to inquire about working with me or sharing your story in our next book.
@m.me/dorrisburch

Facebook Page
https://www.facebook.com/thefabfactoracademy

Instagram
@IAmTheFabulousDorrisBurch

YouTube
https://www.youtube.com/c/dorrisburch

ABOUT THE FABULOUS DORRIS BURCH

THE FABULOUS DORRIS BURCH is a world-renowned thought shaker for women over 40 and beyond Up-Leveling their Visibility. To be seen and heard in your message + movement just by being fully YOU. Through her "The Fab Factor" podcast, transformational coaching program and mastermind for high-level visionary women entrepreneurs, and compiler of the bestselling "Don't Be Invisible Be Fabulous" anthology book series, and her bestselling "The Little Black Book Of Being Fabulous"

book, and her daily free inspirational posts, and videos distributed across her social media channels, for over a decade she has been helping women over 40 to step into the most powerful versions of themselves to be fabulous and design lives and businesses they are wildly obsessed with to create their most fabulous lives. Her mission is for women over 40 and beyond to… Don't Be Invisible. Be Fabulous!

Combining a background in fashion merchandising as well as human resources and metaphysical science with a deep knowledge of spiritual and energetic principles, Fabulous Dorris isn't quite like any other "coach" you've encountered. A true self-made fabulous woman. She credits her success to her sheer determination, a deep desire to liberate others, and an unwavering belief in her own dreams to be seen and heard in a big way.

Fabulous Dorris has earned a master of public affairs in government/business relations, a master of arts in human resources & management and a bachelor of science in fashion merchandising and a bachelor's in metaphysical science. She is currently completing her doctorate in metaphysical science. In addition to many many certifications in coaching and leadership.

She is a native of Kansas City, Missouri, but currently lives in the Chicagoland area with her husband and son.

FAB FACTOR

BY DORRIS BURCH

THIS IS A MOVEMENT OF
F.A.B.U.L.O.U.S. WOMEN

F WOMEN WHO HAVE <u>FAITH</u> THAT MOVES MOUNTAINS

A WOMEN WHO LIVE IN THE <u>AWARENESS</u> OF THEIR INHERENT CREATIVE POWER

B WOMEN WHO <u>BELIEVE</u> ALL THINGS ARE POSSIBLE

U WOMEN WHO GIVE THEMSELVES <u>UNAPOLOGETIC PERMISSION</u> TO BE UNAPOLOGICALLY POWERFUL

L WOMEN WHO <u>LOVE</u> THEMSELVES

O WOMEN WHO KNOW <u>OPULENCE</u> IS THEIR BIRTHRIGHT

U WOMEN WHO ARE IN <u>UNITY</u> WITH THEIR VOICE AND MESSAGE

S WOMEN WHO ARE <u>SPIRITUALLY CONNECTED</u> TO GOD, UNIVERSE & THE COLLECTIVE FORCES SO THEY TRUST / KNOW THEY ARE TAKEN CARE OF NO MATTER WHAT

WHAT IS FABULOUS?

FABULOUS IS
THE EUPHORIC FEELING
THAT ONLY OWNING
YOUR POWER AND LIVING
IT CAN BRING

FABULOUS IS
EVERYTHING YOU EVER WANTED
TO BE, DO AND HAVE.

FAB FACTOR

TheFabFactor.com

Don't Be Invisible. *Be Fabulous!*

Made in the USA
Monee, IL
07 April 2022

6819ea38-9a09-4b53-b079-f10d7a3ac1c1R01